PRAYERS
FOR THE
CHRISTIAN
YEAR

PRAYERS
FOR THE
CHRISTIAN
YEAR

SECOND EDITION
REVISED AND ENLARGED

Prepared by the
Committee on Public Worship and Aids
to Devotion of the General Assembly
of the Church of Scotland

LONDON
OXFORD UNIVERSITY PRESS
GLASGOW   MELBOURNE

Oxford University Press, Amen House, London E.C.4

GLASGOW   NEW YORK   TORONTO   MELBOURNE   WELLINGTON
BOMBAY   CALCUTTA   MADRAS   KARACHI   LAHORE   DACCA
CAPE TOWN   SALISBURY   NAIROBI   IBADAN   ACCRA
KUALA LUMPUR   HONG KONG

First edition   1935
Second edition   1952
Reprinted 1954, 1957, 1960, and 1963

PRINTED IN GREAT BRITAIN

THE observance of the Christian Year ceased in
the Church of Scotland at the Reformation. At
that time there were cogent reasons for such a
departure from ancient custom. With the dis-
appearance, however, of the conditions from which
they derived their force, these reasons have long
since lost their validity. Other conditions have now
emerged which make it desirable that a return
should be made to the general practice of Christen-
dom, on those great occasions when the transcend-
ent facts of the Christian Faith are the subjects of
commemoration.

The chief of these occasions—Christmas, Good
Friday, Easter, and Whitsunday—are everywhere
now identified with public holidays. The Church
would be remiss in its duty if it left them with none
but that secular association, and neglected to use
the appropriate means of impressing their primary
religious significance upon the public mind.

Further, the Church of Scotland believes in the
fellowship of all believers, as implied in the
doctrines of the Holy Catholic Church and the
Communion of Saints. The commemorations
referred to afford it inspiring opportunities of
bearing witness to that element in its faith, by
uniting *ex animo* with the Holy Church throughout

all the world, in celebrating the fundamental certainties which are held in common by all believers.

Moreover, such commemorations serve a great evangelic purpose. They ensure that the basic truths of the faith once for all delivered to the saints shall be adequately proclaimed, not by preaching only, but, on these occasions, by the whole cast and substance of the Church's worship.

Forms of prayer appropriate for such a purpose, and conforming to the usage of the Church of Scotland in its public services, have not hitherto been available. To meet this need, the General Assembly instructed their Committee on Public Worship and Aids to Devotion to prepare the prayers contained in the present book. In draft, they were submitted to the Assembly, and approved. In their completed form it is by no means claimed that they have the perfection of diction which would be necessary to fit them for liturgical use; but for such a use they are not intended. They have been drawn up for the guidance of Ministers in making their own preparation for leading their people's worship, and it is with that end in view that they are now placed at the service of the Church.

*   *   *

MILLAR PATRICK, D.D.
Convener of Editorial Committee

PREFACE TO THE SECOND
EDITION

THE original edition of *Prayers for the Christian Year*, published in 1935, met with a warm welcome from the Church, and obviously was of assistance to many Ministers who wished to impart to their services on the great occasions of the Christian Year the essential note of those occasions. The present edition has been carefully and extensively revised, and additional services have been included. Services are now provided for all the Sundays of Advent and of Lent and fuller provision has been made for Christmas, Good Friday, and Easter. In recent years the observance of the Church's Year has made great progress in Scotland, and it is hoped that these additional services will enable the message of the different seasons to be more fully expressed. The Sundays of Advent and of Lent have each their own message; the mood of the morning of Good Friday and the morning of Easter is different from that of the evening.

Generally, the services are intended to be fitted into the framework of the Morning Service as it is expressed in the *Book of Common Order*. That Service allows of a certain variation in order, and the prayers in this book need not invariably be used in the order in which they are printed. The services for Holy Week fall into a class by themselves.

Lessons and praise are not generally suggested as they are available in the *Book of Common Order* and in *A Year's Praise*, but it was thought that in the Holy Week Services it would be of advantage to incorporate them in the text of the services.

As in the first edition, many sources have been drawn upon in compiling the services. Acknowledgement must be made to those mentioned in the original Preface, viz. *The Liturgy and Other Divine Offices* of the Catholic Apostolic Church, Canon Bright's *Ancient Collects and Other Prayers*, *The Book of Common Prayer*, and Dr. John Hunter's *Devotional Services*. In the Service of Nine Lessons and Carols, the opening bidding prayer follows, by kind permission, that used at King's College, Cambridge, which is published in *Daily Prayer* (O.U.P.). The Committee's thanks are due to Mr. Torquil Macleod for permission to use the late Rev. W. H. Macleod's Meditation on the Seven Words from the Cross in the Good Friday Service, and to the late Dr. James Kirkpatrick for help in framing the Holy Week Services. The matter from the *Book of Common Prayer*, which is Crown copyright, is included by permission.

It is hoped that the use of this book may enrich the services of the sanctuary, and promote the diffusion of the great evangelical truths to which the Christian Year bears witness.

JOHN WILSON BAIRD, D.D.

1951 *Convener of Editorial Committee*

CONTENTS

FIRST SUNDAY
IN ADVENT

OUR God shall come, and shall not keep silence. He shall call to the heavens from above, and to the earth, that He may judge His people. And the heavens shall declare His righteousness: for God is judge Himself.

Blessed is the King that cometh in the name of the Lord: peace in heaven, and glory in the highest.

Blessed are those servants, whom the Lord, when He cometh, shall find watching.

I

ALMIGHTY and everlasting God, who orderest all things in heaven and on earth: we give Thee thanks and praise that Thou didst make all ages a preparation for the coming of Thy Son, our blessed Redeemer. Prepare us for the coming of Him whom Thou dost send, and grant that of His fullness we may all receive; through the same Jesus Christ our Lord. AMEN.

HEAVENLY Father, we acknowledge our unworthiness to come before Thee. We have sinned against Thee, through ingratitude, disobedience, and hardness of heart. We have not heeded the warnings of Thy prophets, nor waited for the appearing of Thy Son. We have loved the world and the things of the world, and have not sought Thy kingdom and righteousness. Wherefore we beseech Thy mercy.

B

Almighty God, have mercy upon us; reckon not against us our transgressions, but pardon our offences. Increase in us Thy heavenly grace, that we may be fortified against all our enemies, visible and invisible, and, being delivered from blindness of heart and wilfulness of sin, be as men who watch for their Lord; through the same Jesus Christ our Lord. AMEN.

O GOD, who hast made us for Thyself; cleanse us of evil, we beseech Thee, in body, soul, and spirit; incline our hearts to Thy testimonies; turn away our eyes from beholding vanity. Help us to live soberly, righteously, and godly in this present world; deliver us from the undue love of earthly things, and set our affections on things above. Take us into Thy care and guidance as we offer and present ourselves to Thee for Thy service; use us as Thou wilt and when Thou wilt, to the good of our fellow men and the glory of Thy holy name. AMEN.

ALMIGHTY God, give us grace that we may cast away the works of darkness, and put upon us the armour of light, now in the time of this mortal life, in which Thy Son Jesus Christ came to visit us in great humility; that in the last day, when He shall come again in His glorious majesty to judge both the quick and the dead, we may rise to the life immortal; through Him who liveth and reigneth with Thee and the Holy Ghost, now and ever. AMEN.

II

ALMIGHTY God, Fountain of light and love; we give Thee thanks and praise for all we owe to Thy guiding and sustaining hand, for the many mercies Thou hast bestowed upon us in the past, and for our assurance that Thy goodness will never fail. Most of all we adore Thee for Thine unspeakable mercy in sending Thine only-begotten Son into the world, that believing on Him we should not perish, but have everlasting life. We magnify Thy name for the fulfilment in Him of the expectation of the ages; and for the increase of His government among the children of men. Grant that we may praise Thee, not only with our lips, but in our lives, serving Thee without fear, in holiness and righteousness, all the days of our life; through Jesus Christ our Lord. AMEN.

O HEAVENLY Father, hear us, as we intercede for our brethren of mankind.

Bless abundantly Thy universal Church. Fill it with all truth, and in all truth with all peace. Where it is corrupt, purify it; where it is in error, direct it; where it is right, strengthen and confirm it; where it is in want, furnish it; where it is divided and rent asunder, in mercy heal and restore it, O Thou Holy One of Israel.

We pray especially for Thy Church in this land. Shed down upon her ministers and people all heavenly wisdom and grace; enlighten them with knowledge of Thy Word; inflame them with a pure zeal for Thy glory; and grant that by their endeavours Thy Church may be comforted and established, and Thy kingdom on earth be strengthened and enlarged.

Almighty God, who rulest over the kingdoms of men; we humbly beseech Thee to bless our native land. We pray for our Sovereign Lady the Queen, and for the members of the Royal House; for the ministers of the Crown, the High Court of Parliament, and all who are set in authority throughout our Empire; that they may order all things in wisdom and righteousness.

O God, the Father of all, who alone makest men to be of one mind; remove, we pray Thee, all causes of strife and contention between nations and classes, and bring to pass the promised reign of Thy Son, the Prince of Peace. Inspire us to break down all oppression and wrong, to gain for every man his due reward, and from every man his due service; that each may live for all and all may care for each.

Almighty Father, who didst send Thy Son to dwell in an earthly home; purify, we beseech Thee, family life in this land and throughout the world, and deepen in us a sense of the worth and sacredness of home. Bless our own loved ones wheresoever they may be, . . . Keep them from sin and danger, and let Thine everlasting arms be ever around them.

O God, the Refuge of the poor, the Hope of the humble, the Salvation of the needy; hear us as we pray for those who are worn by illness, for those who are wronged or oppressed, and for the weary and the heavy-laden, that they may be strengthened by Thy grace, and healed by Thy consolations. Let the Dayspring from on high visit them that sit in darkness and in the shadow of death, to guide their feet into the way of peace; through Jesus Christ our Lord. AMEN.

ALMIGHTY God, who hast brought the living and the departed into one communion of saints; we give Thee hearty thanks for the grace Thou didst bestow upon Thy servants whom Thou hast called out of this world unto Thyself. Encourage us by their example, that we may follow after their goodness, and at the last attain, with them, to the perfect fellowship of Thy heavenly kingdom; through Jesus Christ our Lord, who liveth and reigneth with Thee and the Holy Spirit, one God, world without end. AMEN.

III

ALMIGHTY and Eternal God, whose light hath shined in our mortal darkness; reveal Thy presence in our souls, and direct us in our thoughts and words and deeds; awaken us from the sleep of sin, and make us know that now is the accepted time, and now the day of salvation; through Jesus Christ our Lord. AMEN.

IV

O GOD, who hast taught us that the night is far spent and the day is at hand; grant that we may ever be found watching for the coming of Thy Son. May we wait with patient hope for the day of the Lord, and so abide in Him that, when He shall appear, we may not be ashamed; through the same Jesus Christ our Lord. AMEN.

SECOND SUNDAY
IN ADVENT

This Sunday has for long been associated with the gift of Holy Scripture, and especially with its witness to our Lord.

THE earth shall be full of the knowledge of the Lord as the waters cover the sea.

Repent ye, for the kingdom of heaven is at hand.

Behold the Lord cometh and all His saints with Him; and there shall be in that day a great light.

I

ALMIGHTY God, Father of all, the hope of those who cry unto Thee, receive at Thy throne of light the humble supplication of Thy people, and amid the unwearied praises of Cherubim and Seraphim who stand before Thee, give ear unto our prayers and adoration; through Jesus Christ our Lord. AMEN.

ALMIGHTY God, who in Thy holiness art greatly to be feared; we confess that we have sinned against Thee in thought, in word, and in deed. Thou hast given us Thy word to be a lamp unto our feet and a light unto our path; but we have rejected Thy truth and brought reproach unto Thy holy name. We have received Thy word, but have neglected its message, and the great hope of Thy coming has grown dim in our souls.

Forgive us, good Lord; forgive Thy people who have sinned against Thee. From the shame of sin cover us; from the guilt of sin cleanse us; from the power and dominion of sin deliver us. Heal our souls, that being no longer separated from Thee by our iniquity, we may cleave unto Thee with our whole heart, striving ever to do Thy will and to hasten the coming of Thy kingdom; through Jesus Christ our Lord. AMEN.

[ALMIGHTY God, who art Life eternal, quicken and revive us that we may work Thy works while it is day, knowing that the night cometh when no man can work. Reveal Thy presence to us and keep us ever mindful of Thy judgements upon all that we think or say or do. Shew Thyself unto us amid all the changes of our days, teaching us that in sundry ways and divers manners Thou art still visiting and redeeming Thy people. Grant us the spirit of reverent hope and expectation, that we may prepare ourselves to meet our Lord when He cometh and be found acceptable in His sight; through the same Jesus Christ our Lord. AMEN.]

BLESSED Lord, who hast caused all Holy Scriptures to be written for our learning; Grant that we may in such wise hear them, read, mark, learn, and inwardly digest them, that by patience and comfort of Thy holy word, we may embrace and ever hold fast the blessed hope of everlasting life, which Thou hast given us in our Saviour Jesus Christ. AMEN.

ALMIGHTY God, give us grace that we may cast away the works of darkness, and put upon us the armour of light, now in the time of this mortal life, in which Thy Son Jesus Christ came to visit us in great humility; that in the last day, when He shall come again in His glorious majesty to judge both the quick and the dead, we may rise to the life immortal; through Him who liveth and reigneth with Thee and the Holy Ghost, now and ever. AMEN.

II

WE will extol Thee O God our King, and we will bless Thy name for ever and ever.

ALMIGHTY and everlasting God, we praise Thee for all Thy benefits towards us; for the gifts of creation, the bounties of Providence and the treasures of redeeming love. We thank Thee that in times past Thou didst speak to our fathers by the prophets and in these last days by Thy Son. Especially this day we thank Thee for Thy Holy Word, for the great salvation it makes known to us, and for the light it sheds upon our earthly way. We bless Thee that it gives consolation to the penitent, comfort to the afflicted and to the dying the hope of everlasting life. Grant that, reading its lessons aright, we may be enabled so to order our steps that at the last we may obtain Thy blessed promises; through Him who is the Way, the Truth, and the Life, even Jesus Christ our Lord. AMEN.

ALMIGHTY God our heavenly Father, hear us as we intercede for our brethren of mankind, beseeching Thee to bestow Thy grace as Thou beholdest the wants of Thy children everywhere. We pray for Thy Church; redeem it from all evil and perfect it in Thy love. Purify from their sins all who love Thee and hasten the time when all nations shall serve Thee. Strengthen our faith and kindle our zeal, that we may fervently desire the salvation of all men and labour with greater diligence in the service of Thy kingdom.

We pray for our nation and Empire, that Thou wouldst keep them true to Thee. Bless, we beseech Thee, our Sovereign Lady the Queen and all to whom Thou hast committed the government of this people. Endue them with wisdom and power from above that they may ever seek to do Thy will.

[Lord, bless this kingdom and empire, that religion and virtue may season all sorts of men; that there may be peace within its gates and prosperity in all its borders. In peace so preserve it that it corrupt not; in trouble so defend it that it suffer not; and so order it, whether in plenty or in want, that it may patiently and peaceably seek Thee, the only full supply and sure foundation both of men and states; that so it may continue a place and people to do Thee service to the end of time.]

We pray for the afflicted, for those weighed down by oppression and misery, for the lonely and forsaken, for widows and orphans, for all who mourn. Speak peace to wounded consciences, heal the sick, deliver those who are exposed to temptation or danger, and lead us all by the waters of comfort and the ways of righteousness into Thy peace.

We commend to Thee our loved ones, wheresoever they may be, especially those from whom we are now separated. Protect our dwellings from evil and fill them with holiness, peace, and love; through Jesus Christ our Lord. AMEN.

O LORD most high, with Thy holy Church throughout all the world, we give Thee thanks for all Thy faithful servants, who having witnessed in their lives a good confession, have left the light of their example to shine before Thy people on earth. Mercifully grant that we too may be faithful, so that when our Lord shall come a second time, He may find us diligent in service, and ready to enter with Him into the many mansions of our Father's

house; through Jesus Christ our Lord, who liveth
and reigneth with Thee and the Holy Spirit, one
God, blessed for ever. AMEN.

III

O LORD Jesus Christ, who art the Truth Incarnate, and the Teacher of the faithful; let
Thy Spirit overshadow us as we meditate on Thy
word, and conform our thoughts to Thy revela-
tion, that, learning of Thee with honest hearts, we
may be rooted and built up in Thee; who livest and
reignest with the Father, and the Holy Spirit, ever
one God, world without end. AMEN.

IV

O LORD our God, cause the Sun of Righteousness to arise in our hearts and enlighten us
with the brightness of Thy coming; that we who
rejoice in the word of Thy promise may not be
confounded at Thy appearing to judge the world.
Make us so to walk in the paths of holiness, that
by Thy grace we may live soberly, justly, and tem-
perately in the present world, and in the world to
come obtain everlasting life; through Jesus Christ
our Lord. AMEN.

THIRD SUNDAY
IN ADVENT

*On this day, while recalling that at His first coming our
Lord Jesus Christ sent His messenger before his face
to prepare His way before Him, the Church makes
special remembrance before God of all who are called
to the sacred ministry.*

HOW beautiful upon the mountains are the feet
of him that bringeth good tidings, that publisheth peace; that bringeth good tidings of good,
that publisheth salvation; that saith unto Zion, Thy
God reigneth.

Behold, I will send my messenger, and he shall
prepare the way before Me: and the Lord, whom
ye seek, shall suddenly come to His temple, even
the messenger of the covenant, whom ye delight
in: behold, he shall come, saith the Lord of hosts.

Then said Jesus to them again, Peace be unto
you: as My Father hath sent Me, even so send I you.

I

O LORD God, merciful and holy, who didst
command light to shine out of darkness, who
hast given us rest in sleep, and hast raised us up
to glorify Thee and to declare Thy goodness; we
beseech Thee of Thy great mercy to accept the
worship which we now offer unto Thee, and to
grant unto us our requests for all things needful for
the present life and for our everlasting salvation;
through Jesus Christ our Lord, to whom, with
Thee the Father, and the Holy Spirit, one blessed
Trinity, be all honour, praise, and adoration, world
without end. AMEN.

ALMIGHTY God, Father of our Lord Jesus
Christ, we humbly acknowledge our manifold
sins and offences against Thee in thought, word,
and deed. We have neglected opportunities of good
which in Thy love Thou didst provide for us. We
have been overcome by temptations, from which
Thou wast ready to guard us. We have looked unto
men, and not unto Thee, in doing our daily work,
and have lived in forgetfulness of the life to come.

O Thou, who art ever merciful and gracious to
those who turn to Thee, grant us Thy pardon.
Have mercy upon us, O Almighty God, heavenly
Father, who forgivest iniquity and transgression.
Give us true repentance and sincere faith in Thee,
that we may live more worthy of our Christian
calling, and to the glory of Thy great name,
through Jesus Christ our Lord and Saviour. AMEN.

O LORD Jesus Christ, who at Thy first coming
didst send Thy messenger to prepare Thy way
before Thee; grant that the ministers and stewards
of Thy mysteries may likewise so prepare and make
ready Thy way, by turning the hearts of the disobedient to the wisdom of the just, that at Thy
second coming to judge the world we may be found
an acceptable people in Thy sight; who livest and
reignest with the Father and the Holy Spirit, ever
one God, world without end. AMEN.

ALMIGHTY God, give us grace that we may
cast away the works of darkness, and put upon
us the armour of light, now in the time of this
mortal life, in which Thy Son Jesus Christ came to
visit us in great humility; that in the last day, when
He shall come again in His glorious Majesty to
judge both the quick and the dead, we may rise to

the life immortal, through Him who liveth and
reigneth with Thee and the Holy Ghost, now and
ever. AMEN.

II

O ALMIGHTY Father, from whom cometh
down every good and every perfect gift, we
humbly thank Thee for all Thy mercies. We thank
Thee for our creation, preservation, and redemption; for all Thy gifts of nature and of grace; for
health and strength; for homes and kindred; for
true friends and wise teachers; for all the blessings
of this life, and for our hope of a better life to come.
Most of all at this time do we adore Thee for Thine
infinite goodness in sending Thine only-begotten
Son into the world, that we, believing in Him, may
not perish, but have everlasting life. We thank
Thee that when He ascended up on high, He gave
to the Church the gift of the sacred ministry, and
we pray Thee for grace rightly to use this and all
Thy gifts, so that through the power and grace of
His first coming into the world, we may be ready
to meet Him when He comes again to judge the
world; through the same Jesus Christ our Lord.
AMEN.

O GOD, who hast taught us by Thy holy Apostle
to make prayers and supplications for all men,
be pleased to hear our humble intercessions which
in the name of Thine eternal Son we offer unto Thee.

Almighty God, who hast built Thy Church on
the foundation of the Apostles and prophets, Jesus
Christ Himself being the chief corner-stone; preserve Thy people in the true faith, and perfect
them into one living Temple of the Holy Spirit;
and grant that Thy Church may be a refuge for the

sinful, a shelter for the oppressed, and a house of prayer for all nations.

O Lord, we beseech Thee to raise up for the work of the ministry, faithful and able men who shall count it joy to spend and be spent for the souls for which Thy Son did shed His most precious blood, and we pray Thee to fit them for their holy duties by Thy bountiful grace and heavenly benediction.

Most merciful Father, we beseech Thee to bless Thy servants who preach the Gospel to those in darkness. Give them faith and courage, health and strength, and let Thy light shine through them that the knowledge of Thy Son be everywhere brought into dark and ignorant lives.

O Lord our God, who hast given us this land wherein to dwell; we beseech Thee to pour out Thy blessing upon our country, its government, and its people. Grant Thy Holy Spirit to the Queen, and all who are in authority under her, that they may govern in Thy faith and fear, striving to put down evil, and to establish what is good. Preserve both our government and people from the spirit of ambition and pride, and teach us to seek peace at home and peace with all nations, to the glory of Thy holy name.

O God, who dost not willingly afflict the children of men, look in compassion upon all in misery. Have mercy on ignorant souls, to instruct them; on deluded minds, to enlighten them; on broken hearts, to heal them; on the tempted, to strengthen them; on the fallen, to raise them. O blessed Jesus, who didst shed for men Thy precious blood, look upon all in Thy tender mercy and save them for thine own name's sake, even Jesus Christ our Saviour. AMEN.

O ETERNAL God, with whom do rest the spirits of the just made perfect, we thank Thee for all Thy servants departed this life in Thy faith and fear; for all who have loved us and toiled for us; for all who have brought blessing to their fellow-men by their charity and sacrifice; for all who have preached Thy word, administered Thy sacraments, and carried Thy gospel to lighten the dark places of the earth; for all who have suffered for righteousness' sake. Let their example and memory ever be an inspiration to us, that we, following in their steps, may with them receive the crown of life; through Jesus Christ our Lord, who liveth and reigneth with Thee and the Holy Spirit, one God, world without end. AMEN.

III

ALMIGHTY God, who hast instructed Thy Church with heavenly teaching, and hast caused the light of Thy glorious gospel to shine into the world; enlighten our hearts with the truth of Thy word, that we may ponder and love those things that are pleasing to Thee; through Jesus Christ our Lord. AMEN.

IV

MOST Gracious God, we beseech Thee, let not Thy word return unto Thee void. Bless to our souls the preaching of Thy Gospel. Perfect the faith of us who believe, and sow the good seed in the hearts of them who believe not; that we, being rooted and grounded in Thy holy word, may bring forth good fruit abundantly; through Jesus Christ our Lord, to whom with Thee the Father and the Holy Ghost be glory now and ever. AMEN.

FOURTH SUNDAY
IN ADVENT

THERE shall come a star out of Jacob, and a
sceptre shall rise out of Israel.

The night is far spent, and the day is at hand; let
us therefore cast off the works of darkness, and let
us put upon us the armour of light.

Let your loins be girded about and your lights
burning; and ye yourselves like unto men that
wait for their Lord.

I

LORD God Almighty, King of glory and love
eternal, worthy art Thou at all times to receive
adoration, praise, and blessing; but especially at
this time do we praise Thee for the sending of
Thy Son our Saviour Jesus Christ, for whom our
hearts do wait, and to whom, with Thee and the
Holy Spirit, one God, be honour and dominion,
now and for ever. AMEN.

REJECT us not, O God our Saviour, though we
be laden with many sins, remembered and forgotten, wrought against Thee, against our brother,
and against our own souls. Teach us by Thy Holy
Spirit rightly to weigh our offences and earnestly
to repent of them. Day by day we have offended in
thought and intention, in word and in deed. Our
consciences accuse us; our sins witness against
us: and we know that Thou art a most righteous
Judge.

Forgive us our sins, O Lord, and make us to

abhor them with our whole heart; that at the coming of Thy Son our Lord, we may be enabled to receive His gifts of peace, love, and truth; through the same Jesus Christ our Lord. AMEN.

O CHRIST our God, who wilt come to judge the world in the Manhood which Thou hast assumed, we pray Thee to sanctify us wholly, that in the day of Thy Coming our whole spirit, soul, and body may so attain to a fresh life in Thee, that we may live and reign with Thee for ever.

O Wisdom, that camest out of the mouth of the Most High, reaching from one end to another, mightily and sweetly ordering all things; come to teach us the way of understanding.

O Lord and Leader of the House of Israel, who didst appear to Moses in the flame of the burning bush, and gavest the law on Sinai; come to deliver us with an outstretched arm.

O root of Jesse, who standest for an ensign to the people; before whom kings shall shut their mouths, whom the nations shall entreat; come to deliver us now, tarry not.

O Key of David, and Sceptre of the House of Israel, who openest and no man shutteth, and shuttest and no man openeth; come Thou, and bring forth from the prison-house him that is bound.

O Dayspring from on high, brightness of eternal light, Sun of righteousness; come Thou, and shine in upon them that are sitting in darkness and in the shadow of death.

O King of the Gentiles, God of Israel, Thou corner-stone that makest both one; come Thou, and save Thy creatures, whom Thou didst fashion from the dust of the earth.

O Emmanuel, our King and Lawgiver, the expectation of the Gentiles, and their desire; come to save us, O Lord, our Saviour and our God. AMEN.

Or,

ALMIGHTY God, we beseech Thee, grant unto Thy people grace that they may wait with vigilance for the advent of Thy Son our Lord; that, when He shall arise from Thy right hand to visit the earth in righteousness and Thy people with salvation, He may find us, not sleeping in sin, but diligent in His service and rejoicing in His praises; that so we may enter in with Him unto the marriage of the Lamb; for the merits of the same Jesus Christ our Lord. AMEN.

Or,

O LORD, raise up (we pray Thee) Thy power, and come among us, and with great might succour us; that whereas, through our sins and wickedness, we are sore let and hindered in running the race that is set before us, Thy bountiful grace and mercy may speedily help and deliver us; through the satisfaction of Thy Son our Lord, to whom with Thee and the Holy Ghost be honour and glory, world without end. AMEN.

And,

ALMIGHTY God, give us grace that we may cast away the works of darkness, and put upon us the armour of light, now in the time of this mortal life, in which Thy Son Jesus Christ came to visit us in great humility; that in the last day, when He shall come again in His glorious Majesty to judge both the quick and the dead, we may rise to the life immortal; through Him who liveth and reigneth with Thee and the Holy Ghost, now and ever. AMEN.

II

GREAT art Thou, O Lord, and greatly to be praised; Thy greatness is unsearchable. One generation shall praise Thy works to another and shall declare Thy mighty acts.

WE praise and adore Thee, O God, our Father, who willest not that any should perish, but that all should come unto Thee and live. We praise Thee for sending Thy Son as at this time to be the Saviour of the world, that we might be brought back from all our wanderings to our Father's house. We praise Thee for sending forth Thy Spirit into our hearts; for Thy Church into which Thou hast brought us; and for all the helps, comforts, and blessings which we have received from Thy fatherly hand.

Bless the Lord, O my soul, and all that is within me, bless His holy name.

Bless the Lord, O my soul, and forget not all his benefits. Praise be to Thee, O God, world without end. AMEN.

HEAR, O Lord, the prayers we offer unto Thee on behalf of others.

O Thou who hast founded a Church for Thyself and hast promised to dwell in it for ever, enlighten and sanctify it, we beseech Thee, by Thy Word and Spirit. Bless all who minister in Thy Church, and increase in them Thy grace, that with joy and assurance they may guard and feed Thy sheep, looking to the great Shepherd and Bishop of souls. Bless all who serve Thee in the rule of Thy

Church; in the care of Thy poor; in the ministry
of Thy praise; and in the teaching of the young.
Strengthen them in their labours; give them courage
to witness a good confession; and cause Thy
Church to increase more and more, that every knee
may bow before Thee, and every tongue confess
that Jesus Christ is Lord.

O God, who rulest in righteousness over the
whole earth; bless, we beseech Thee, all the nations
of the world, and guide the hearts of kings and
rulers, so that equity and peace may everywhere
prevail. Shew Thy favour to our beloved land: continue and increase to us the blessings we enjoy in this
realm. Endow with the light and power of Thy Spirit
those who rule over us. Bless Thy servant Elizabeth
our Queen and all her house, and grant to all men
and women in stations of authority or influence to
discharge their duties to Thy glory, and for the
good of those over whom Thou hast placed them.

We commend to Thee our families and our
children. Dwell in our homes, we beseech Thee;
protect them from all evil, both outwardly and inwardly, and fill them with holiness and peace. We
pray for all dear to us wheresoever they be, that
they may be guarded amidst the dangers of this
present life, and kept by Thy grace unto life eternal.

We pray for the afflicted, for those weighed down
by oppression and misery, for widows and orphans,
and for all who are solitary and forsaken. We entreat Thee to raise up the sick, to comfort those
who are in pain of body or bitterness of soul, and
to deliver those who are in temptation; through
Jesus Christ our Lord. AMEN.

ETERNAL God, in whom the spirits of just men
after they die do rest in peace; we bless and praise

Thy holy name for all Thy servants departed this life in Thy faith and fear, and especially for those most dear to us, of whom we have good hope that they are fallen asleep in Jesus. Help us so to lift up our eyes to that better land where there is no separation or grief or sin, that even here we may be united with them in fellowship of spirit, and that finally we may be gathered together with them in Thy blessed presence; through Jesus Christ our Lord, to whom, with the Father and the Holy Ghost, be glory now and ever. AMEN.

III

O LORD God Almighty, the King of Glory, who art our true peace, and love eternal; enlighten our souls with the brightness of Thy peace, and purify our consciences with the sweetness of Thy love, that we may with peaceful hearts wait for the Author of peace, and in the adversities of this world may ever have Thee for our Guardian and Protector. AMEN.

IV

GRANT, we beseech Thee, Almighty God, that the solemn feast of our redemption which is now at hand, may both help us in this present life, and further us towards the attaining of Thine eternal joy in that which is to come; through Jesus Christ our Lord. AMEN.

These words following may, if desired, precede the Blessing.

MAY the Lord Jesus Christ, who by His most blessed Advent deigned to relieve the world, sanctify your minds and bodies.

May He grant you by the virtue of the Holy Spirit to understand the precepts of His law, that ye may be able to await His second coming without fear.

May He so free you from all guilt, that when He cometh, He may not examine you in wrath, but take you to His reward in glory.

CHRISTMAS EVE

LIGHT is sown for the righteous, and gladness for the upright in heart. Rejoice in the Lord, ye righteous; and give thanks at the remembrance of His holiness.

The desire of all nations shall come: and I will fill this house with glory, saith the Lord of Hosts.

Sanctify yourselves; for tomorrow the Lord will do wonders among you.

I

ETERNAL God, our heavenly Father, who hast caused light to shine out of darkness; shine now in our hearts, we beseech Thee, to give the light of the knowledge of Thy glory in the face of Jesus Christ.

Blessed Saviour, by Thy divine humility and lowly state quicken in us meekness, wonder, and penitence.

Holy Spirit, help us now to worship with joy in the beauty of holiness.

And to Thee, O blessed Trinity, be glory, honour, and majesty, world without end. AMEN.

ALMIGHTY God, the Creator and Redeemer of the world, who in the fullness of time didst send Thy Son as an infant of days to seek and to save that which was lost; look in mercy upon us Thine unworthy children. Grant that we, being humbled by Thine infinite love, may freely confess our sins, and receive Thy gracious forgiveness. Make us to rejoice in the wondrous redemption from the power of sin and death, which by the holy incarnation of Thy Son our Saviour Thou dost seal unto us now and forever. Enable us, we pray Thee, more truly to apprehend the great salvation wrought for us, that we may make this Christmastide a glory to Thy name, a season of joy for others, and a pattern of the Christian life on earth; through the same Thy Son, Jesus Christ our Lord. AMEN.

MOST merciful God, for whose chosen handmaid and her Holy Babe there was no room in the inn at Bethlehem; help us all by Thy Spirit to make more room for the Christ in our common days, that His peace and joy may fill our hearts, and His love flow through our lives to the blessing of others, for His name's sake. AMEN.

O GOD, who at this holy season dost bring delight unto Thy little ones by gifts, good cheer, and the lovingkindness of friends; grant that, as their hearts are gladdened to receive the bounty of our earthly love they may come to know Thy divine love in Jesus Christ our Lord and Saviour. AMEN.

O GOD, who makest us glad by the yearly expectation of our Redemption; grant that rejoicing we may receive Thy blessed Son as our Redeemer, and with sure confidence behold Him when He cometh to be our Judge; who liveth and reigneth with Thee and the Holy Spirit, world without end. AMEN.

II

O GOD, who as on this night, by a glorious company of the Heavenly Host, didst proclaim the birth of Thy Son our Saviour upon earth; with heart and voice we join in their holy song, praising

Thee and saying, Glory to God in the highest, and on earth peace, goodwill toward men.

For the heavenly message of peace we thank Thee, O God. Grant, we beseech Thee, that the spirit of reconciliation may prevail ever more widely in the earth, that wars may cease, and that men and nations everywhere may learn to live together in goodwill and brotherly service under the banner of the Prince of Peace.

For all poets and makers of music, who have set forth in beauty and truth the purpose of Thy love in the Babe of Bethlehem, we praise Thee, O God.

O Lord Jesus Christ, whom, in Thy manger-cradle, beasts of field and stall beheld; we thank Thee for the beauty, wonder, and companionship of God's animal creatures. Teach us always to treat them kindly and to spare them pain, for Thy mercy's sake.

For all Thy mercies more than can be numbered we praise Thee, O God, but especially for the blessings of motherhood, of childhood, and of home, for ever hallowed by the light of Bethlehem.

Heavenly Father, who by Thine angel didst call Thy handmaid, Mary, to be the mother of Thy Son; we praise Thee for her, blessed among women. We thank Thee for all that mothers have been to men, guiding their hearts to Thee, and teaching them tenderness and purity, chivalry and love. For mothers of today we pray that by Thy Spirit Thou wilt show them the glory of their calling. To those approaching motherhood give grace, O God, so to esteem Thy gift that they may indeed be temples of Thy Holy Spirit.

For the precious gift of children we thank Thee; and we pray for all who teach and train the young, that their endeavours may be furthered by Thy blessing.

For our own homes we thank Thee and pray that they may be dwellings fit for Thee, and abounding in love and joy and peace. We commend to Thy gracious care our dear ones far from home this night, especially those in any danger. With Thy protection, Lord, give them the knowledge of our love and prayers; and in Thy good time bring them home again in peace; through Jesus Christ our Lord. AMEN.

O GOD, who preservest the souls of Thy servants; we praise Thee for the multitude of the redeemed who have inherited Thy promises, especially for our own beloved who rejoice with Thy saints in heaven. Keep, Lord, our love for them pure and steadfast, our communion of spirit with them strong and true, until we also receive the end of our faith, and are reunited with them in Thy heavenly home.

We beseech Thee to hear us in all these our prayers, for the sake of Jesus Christ Thy Son our Saviour, who with Thee, O Father, and the Holy Ghost, is for ever to be glorified and adored, world without end. AMEN.

III

O GOD of truth and love, by whom is shed the light of Thine incarnate Word, illumine our minds as we ponder the work of our redemption, that Christ may dwell in our hearts by faith, and be shewed forth in our lives by deeds of love done in His name. AMEN.

IV

WATCH Thou, dear Lord, with those who wake, or watch, or weep this night, and give

Thine angels charge over those who sleep. Tend the sick; rest the weary; bless the dying; soothe the suffering; pity thine afflicted; shield thy joyous; and all for Thy Love's sake. AMEN.

O GOD of unchangeable power and eternal light, look favourably on Thy whole Church, that wonderful and sacred mystery; and, by the tranquil operation of Thy perpetual Providence, carry out the work of man's salvation. Let the whole world feel and see that things which were cast down are being raised up, that those which had grown old are being made new, and that all things are returning to perfection; Through Him from whom they took their origin, even Jesus Christ Thy Son our Lord. AMEN.

O GOD, who hast made this most holy night to shine with the brightness of the True Light; grant, we beseech Thee that, as we have known the mystery of that Light upon earth, we may also perfectly enjoy it in heaven; through the same Jesus Christ our Lord, to whom, with the Father and the Holy Spirit, three persons and one God, be glory and dominion for ever. AMEN.

These words, if desired, may precede the Blessing.

MAY God Almighty, who by the incarnation of His only-begotten Son, drove away the darkness of the world, and by His glorious birth enlightened this most holy night, drive away from us the darkness of sin, and enlighten our hearts with the light of Christian grace.

And may He who willed that the great day of His most holy birth should be told by an angel to the shepherds, pour upon us the refreshing shower of His blessing, and guide us, Himself being our shepherd, to the pastures of everlasting joy.

And may He, who through His incarnation united earthly things with heavenly, fill us with the sweetness of inward peace and goodwill, and make us partakers with the heavenly host.

CHRISTMAS DAY

BEHOLD, I bring you good tidings of great joy, which shall be to all people. For unto you is born this day in the city of David, a Saviour, which is Christ the Lord.

Let us now go even unto Bethlehem, and see this thing which is come to pass.

Then shall be sung the Hymn, O come, all ye faithful.

UNTO us a child is born: unto us a son is given. Glory to God in the highest, and on earth peace, goodwill toward men.

I

GLORY to God in the highest, and on earth peace, goodwill toward men. Glory be to Thee, O Father Almighty, who didst command the light to shine out of darkness, and by the incarnation and glorious nativity of Thine only-begotten Son hast shined into our hearts, to give the light of the knowledge of Thy glory in the face of Jesus Christ. Glory be to Thee, O Lord Jesus Christ, Eternal God, who as on this day wast born into the world for us, in all things like unto Thy brethren, that Thou mightest redeem us from sin and evil, and make us sons of God. Glory be to Thee, O Holy Spirit, who hast quickened us together with Christ, and dost conform us to His likeness. All glory and thanks, dominion and power, be unto Thee, O blessed and undivided Trinity, one God eternal, world without end. AMEN.

O GOD, who of Thy tender compassion towards the human race didst send thine only-begotten Son, that He might take upon Him our flesh and dwell amongst us; we worship before the infinite greatness of Thy love. Our hearts are filled with joy, our tongues with praise. O Blessed Saviour, who as on this day wast born in Bethlehem, and didst lie a weak and helpless Child, while yet Thou wast the Eternal Son of God; look upon us, in Thy tender grace, and make us partakers of Thy meekness and humility. O Thou who art the Prince of Peace, grant us that peace which Thou alone canst give, and help us to live at peace with all men; for Thine own name's sake. AMEN.

BLESSED Lord Jesus, we come to Thy cradle, knowing that we are unworthy to approach Thee. Make us pure in heart, that we may see Thee; cleanse and inspire our lives, that we may offer them unto Thee without shame; give us grace to follow the example of Thy great humility, that so we may serve Thee by serving our brethren; who, with the Father and the Holy Spirit, liveth and reigneth, one God, world without end. AMEN.

ALMIGHTY God, who hast given us Thy only-begotten Son Jesus Christ to take our nature upon Him, and as at this time to be born of a pure Virgin; grant that we being regenerate, and made Thy children by adoption and grace, may daily be renewed by Thy Holy Spirit; through the same our Lord Jesus Christ, who liveth and reigneth with Thee and the same Spirit, ever one God, world without end. AMEN.

II

O LORD our God, who didst send Thy Son to be the Saviour of the world; we beseech Thee that the knowledge of Thy salvation may go out to all lands, till in every place Thy name be worshipped and glorified.

Bless Thy Church throughout the world and strengthen her to proclaim the good news of Jesus Christ. Grant that Thy people everywhere may be led to lay the gifts of their adoration and service at the cradle of Thine incarnate Son.

Eternal God, in whose perfect kingdom no sword is drawn but the sword of righteousness, and no strength known but the strength of love; we pray Thee so mightily to shed and spread abroad Thy Spirit, that all peoples and ranks may be gathered under one banner of the Prince of Peace, as children of one God and Father of all.

We beseech Thy favour for our country, with its dominions and dependencies. Bless the Queen and the Royal Family, and all men and women in stations of authority or influence. Bring nigh Thy salvation to all, that glory may dwell in our land. Give us that which is good, that our land may yield her increase. Let righteousness and peace be upon us, that we may walk in the steps of our Saviour.

O God who by giving Thy Son to be born of Mary didst sanctify motherhood and exalt the families of earth; we pray for Thy blessing on our homes, our kindred, and our friends. Make all hearts glad in human fellowship at this time. Let all children be dear to us for the sake of the Holy Child. Let them rejoice in His love as they keep the feast, and give us the childlike heart, that we may share their joy. We remember all who are absent from their homes, that they may be of one heart with us in love, and rejoice with us in Christ the Saviour.

O God of pity, hear us as we remember those for whom the joy of this day is shadowed; the poor, the lonely, the unloved, and those who have no helper. Let those who know Thy love abound in sympathy and kindness, that, having freely received, they may also freely give. Remember in Thy mercy the infirm and the aged, the sick and the sad, the heavy-laden and all who mourn. According to their several necessities and wants, reveal Thyself to them in succour; through Jesus Christ our Redeemer. AMEN.

O LORD Jesus Christ, who redeemest the souls of Thy servants; we praise Thee for the multitude which no man can number, who trod the way of life before us with a hope in their hearts which is now fulfilled. We make special remembrance before Thee at this time of those dear to ourselves who once shared our joy in Thy nativity, and now rejoice with Thy saints in heaven. Keep our love for them true and steadfast, until we receive with them the end of our faith, even life for evermore. And unto Thee, O Lord Jesus Christ, with the Father and the Holy Spirit, one God, be honour and glory for ever and ever. AMEN.

III

O ALMIGHTY God, who by the birth of Thy Holy One into the world as on this day didst give Thy true light to dawn upon our darkness; grant that as Thou hast given us in this time present to believe in the mystery of His incarnation, and hast made us partakers of the divine nature, so in the world to come we may ever abide with Him in the glory of His kingdom; through the same Jesus Christ our Lord. AMEN.

IV

MERCIFUL and most loving God, by whose will and bountiful gift Thine Eternal Son humbled Himself that He might exalt mankind, and became flesh that He might renew in us the Divine image; perfect us in Thy likeness, and bring us at last to rejoice in beholding Thy beauty, and, with all Thy saints, to glorify Thy grace; through the same Jesus Christ our Lord. AMEN.

These words, if desired, may precede the Blessing.

MAY our Lord Jesus Christ bless us, who of old on this day gloriously appeared to the shepherds in the manger.

May He Himself protect and defend us in all things, who for us mercifully took upon Himself our human infancy.

And may He, who is our Lord and Saviour, vouchsafe graciously to preserve us to all eternity. AMEN.

A SERVICE OF NINE LESSONS
AND CAROLS FOR
CHRISTMAS-TIDE

Where possible, the lessons may be read by representatives of Church organizations, the Minister reading the last lesson.

The service shall open with praise, after which, the Congregation still standing, the Minister shall bid them to prayer in these, or like, words:

BELOVED in Christ, at this Christmas-tide let it be our care and delight to hear again the message of the Angels, and in heart and mind to go even unto Bethlehem, and see this thing which is come to pass.

Therefore let us read and mark in Holy Scripture the tale of the loving purpose of God from the first days of our disobedience unto the glorious Redemption brought us by this Holy Child.

But first, let us pray for the needs of the whole world; for peace on earth and goodwill among all His people; for unity and brotherhood within the Church He came to build, and especially in this our own Communion.

And because this would rejoice His heart, let us remember, in His name, the poor and helpless, the cold and hungry, and the oppressed; the sick and them that mourn, the lonely and the unloved, the aged and the little children; all those who know not the Lord Jesus, or who love Him not, or who by sin have grieved His heart.

Lastly, let us remember before God all those

who rejoice with us, but upon another shore, and in a greater light, that multitude which no man can number, whose hope was in the Word made flesh, and with whom in the Lord Jesus we are one for evermore.

Let us pray.

ALMIGHTY God, we pray for the peace of the whole world, and the salvation of all men, beseeching Thee to enlighten the darkness of the earth with the beams of that Sun which shall no more go down. We pray for Thy holy Church, beseeching Thee to grant unto her that peace and unity which are agreeable to Thy will. Regard in Thy mercy the Church of our fathers and grant that all her members may live in concord, and strive together to advance Thy kingdom. Remember, O Lord, our beloved country; give us peace and prosperity, and establish us in righteousness. Remember, O Lord, at this season of joy, all those who are in any kind of sorrow or distress, in particular any such known to ourselves, and help us in our gladness to remember the needs of others.

Blessed Lord Jesus, receive us this day at Thy manger cradle; accept the gifts we bring to Thee; inspire our lives with that love which brought Thee to dwell amongst us in low estate. Help us to live ever in accordance with Thy mind and will, that Thy kingdom upon earth may be revealed in all its glory.

Almighty God, we bless and praise Thy name for all Thy servants departed this life in Thy faith and fear, remembering in especial before Thee those dear to ourselves with whom we were wont to rejoice together at this time, and who now rejoice with Thee in heaven. Keep us ever united with them in spirit, and grant in Thy mercy that at the last we may meet with them again in Thy blessed presence; through Jesus Christ our Lord, to whom with Thee, O Father, and the Holy Ghost, be glory now and ever. AMEN.

Here shall follow the Nine Lessons, with Christmas hymns or carols between. At the beginning of each lesson shall be said the words given below.

1st Lesson: God declareth in the garden of Eden that the seed of woman shall bruise the serpent's head: Genesis iii. 13–15.

2nd Lesson: God promiseth to Abraham that in his seed shall all the nations of the earth be blessed: Genesis xxii. 15–18.

3rd Lesson: Christ's birth and kingdom are foretold by the prophet Isaiah: Isaiah ix. 2, 6, 7.

4th Lesson: The prophet Micah foretelleth the glory of Bethlehem: Micah v. 2–4.

5th Lesson: The Angel Gabriel visiteth the Blessed Virgin Mary: St. Luke i. 26–33, 38.

The Magnificat *may be sung after the 5th Lesson.*

6th Lesson: St. Matthew telleth of Christ's nativity: St. Matthew i. 18–23.

7th Lesson: The shepherds go unto the manger: St. Luke ii. 8–16.

8th Lesson: The Wise Men are led by the star to Jesus: St. Matthew ii. 1–11.

9th Lesson: St. John unfoldeth the mystery of the Incarnation: St. John i. 1–14.

All may stand during the reading of the 9th Lesson.

Then shall the Minister say:

THE Lord bless to us this wondrous record of His love, and to His name be praise.

Then shall be sung the hymn O come, all ye faithful.

After which a Sermon may be preached, and the offerings received. Then shall be said:

T HE Lord be with you;
And with thy spirit.
Lift up your hearts;
We lift them up unto the Lord.
Let us give thanks unto our Lord God;
It is meet and right so to do.

I T is verily meet, right, and our bounden duty, that we should at all times and in all places give thanks unto Thee, O Holy Lord, Father Almighty, Everlasting God; who didst create the heavens and the earth and all that is therein; who didst make man in thine own image:

For that by the mystery of the Word made flesh the light of Thy glory hath shone anew upon the eyes of our mind; so that while we acknowledge Him as God seen by men, we may be drawn by Him to the love of things unseen:

Thee, mighty God, heavenly King, we magnify and praise, with Angels and Archangels, and with all the company of heaven, we worship and adore Thy glorious name; evermore praising Thee, and saying:

H OLY, Holy, Holy, Lord God of Hosts, Heaven and earth are full of Thy glory; Glory be to Thee, O Lord Most High. AMEN.[1]

[1] These words may be sung to the setting in the Church Hymnary No. 713.

O GOD who makest us glad with the yearly remembrance of the birth of Thine only Son, Jesus Christ; grant that as we joyfully receive Him for our Redeemer, so we may with sure confidence behold Him when He shall come to be our Judge; who liveth and reigneth with Thee and the Holy Ghost, world without end. AMEN.

O GOD, who by the leading of a star didst manifest Thine only-begotten Son to the Gentiles; mercifully grant that we, who know Thee now by faith, may after this life be brought to contemplate the beauty of Thy majesty; through the same Jesus Christ our Lord, who liveth and reigneth with Thee and the Holy Ghost, world without end. AMEN.

T HESE prayers we humbly offer up to the throne of heaven in the words which Christ Himself hath taught us:

OUR Father . . .

Then a hymn is sung, and the service is closed with the Benediction.

SUNDAY AFTER CHRISTMAS

GLORY to God in the highest, and on earth peace, good will toward men.

For unto us a Child is born, unto us a Son is given: and the government shall be upon His shoulder: and His name shall be called Wonderful, Counsellor, The mighty God, The everlasting Father, The Prince of Peace. Of the increase of His government and peace there shall be no end.

In this was manifested the love of God toward us, because that God sent His only begotten Son into the world, that we might live through Him.

I

ALMIGHTY God our heavenly Father who hast given us this season of holy joy, we bow before Thee with adoring reverence and lift up our hearts with thankful praise. Fill us, we beseech Thee, with the gladness of Thy great redemption and enable us to join in the angels' song 'Glory to God in the highest and on earth peace, good will toward men'; through Jesus Christ our Lord. AMEN.

O HOLY and Merciful Father, who didst send Thy Son to seek and to save the lost; we confess that we have not always lived in the light Thou gavest us in Him. We have known to do good, but have not done it. Thou hast called to us in the needs of our neighbour, but we have often passed by on the other side. We acknowledge our unworthiness of Thy love incarnate in Jesus, yet we beseech Thee to forgive the iniquity of Thy servants. Blessed be Thy holy name for the comforting assurance of Thy holy Word to all who repent and believe: God so loved the world that He gave His only-begotten Son, that whosoever believeth in Him should not perish but have everlasting life. Fulfil in us Thy word, we beseech Thee, and forgive and cleanse us from all our sins; through the same Jesus Christ our Saviour. AMEN.

O LORD our God, who by the birth of Thy Son Jesus Christ hast given us a great light to dawn on our darkness; grant that as we welcome our Redeemer, His presence may shed abroad in our hearts and in our homes the light of heavenly peace and joy. Help us to celebrate this season in humility and gratitude, in unselfish love and cheerful service, and that it may be a blessing to our souls, a benefit to those around us and a thanksgiving to Thee; through the same Jesus Christ our Lord. AMEN.

O IMMORTAL Lord God who inhabitest eternity, and hast brought us, Thine unworthy servants, to the close of another year; pardon, we most humbly beseech Thee, our transgressions in the past, and graciously abide with us all the days of our life; guard and direct us in all trials and temptations, that by Thy blessing we may grow in grace as we grow in years, and at the last may finish our course with joy; through Jesus Christ our Lord, who liveth and reigneth with Thee and the Holy Spirit, world without end. AMEN.

II

THE Lord hath done great things for us whereof we are glad.

WE praise Thee O God, for great is Thy mercy toward us. Thou hast made us in Thine own image, and hast given us minds to know Thee, hearts to love Thee, and wills to serve Thee. In goodness art Thou exalted, O Lord, and Thy tender mercies are over all Thy works.

We thank Thee for this day of rest and worship and for all the hallowed memories it enshrines. Help us to hold it fast as Thy gift and to keep it holy unto Thee.

We praise Thee for the kindness of others, whereby the path of life has been made more easy for us, for the blessedness of home, for the joy of friendship, and for the tenderness which links us to our dear ones on earth and in heaven.

Most of all do we magnify Thee for Thy greatest gift, and bless Thee that in the fullness of time Thou didst give the light of the knowledge of Thy glory in the face of Jesus Christ. As our hearts turn to Bethlehem and to the Child in the Manger we adore Thee as the Giver of Thine unspeakable gift, and we bless Thee for that Thou hast indeed visited and redeemed Thy people.

Almighty God, our Heavenly Father, in whom all men are one family, hear us as in the name of Christ we intercede for our brethren of mankind. Be gracious to Thy holy Church here and everywhere. Endow her plenteously with Thy Holy Spirit. Have pity on those who are in the darkness of ignorance and error, and bring them to Thy light.

We pray for all the nations of the earth, that Thou wouldst lead them in the paths of peace and brotherhood. Let the spirit of Christmas be increasingly spread abroad that those who have been offended may forgive, and those who have offended their brethren may repent, and all Thy children be brought into one spirit, praising and loving Thee.

We ask for Thy blessing on our country with its dominions and dependencies. Bestow Thy favour on our Queen, and all the Royal Family. Give grace and wisdom to all in authority under the Queen and over us. Let righteousness, kindness and goodwill be shed throughout the land by love of Christ the Lord.

Our Heavenly Father, whose holy Child Jesus is born unto us; we entreat Thee that in memory of His infancy, and of the love He bore unto Thy little ones, all children may be precious in our eyes. Make us heedful and helpful in our dealings with them. Let Thy love be felt in every home, and let our gifts one to another be a reminder of Thee who givest all.

Be with those who at this season are sick or sad or suffering, the poor, the lonely, the homeless, the distressed, and those who are mourning their dear ones. Speak peace to troubled souls, and raise up all who are bowed down.

We pray for our own loved ones, wheresoever they may be, especially for those who are far away; give Thine angels charge concerning them, and keep them under the shadow of Thy wings.

O Lord, in whom all souls live, we thank Thee for those whom Thou hast called from this earthly life to Thy Heavenly presence, and pray that by Thy grace we may be brought to enjoy with them the many mansions of our Father's House; through Jesus Christ our Lord, who liveth and reigneth with Thee and the Holy Spirit, one God, world without end. AMEN.

III

O LORD our God, the source of all knowledge and the fountain of all wisdom; grant that our speaking and hearing may be guided by Thy Spirit unto Thee. May all that is not in accordance with Thy will perish in the utterance, and all that is true be preserved for the good of Thy people, the extension of Thy kingdom, and the glory of Thy holy Name; through Jesus Christ our Lord. AMEN.

IV

A LMIGHTY God, who didst send Thy Son to be the Light of the world; we pray Thee that in His light we may see light clearly. Bestow upon us all, we beseech Thee, gifts of love and good will, that the likeness of Thy Son may be found in us, and that we may ever set forth Thy glory; through the same Jesus Christ our Lord. AMEN.

EVENING SERVICE: LAST SUNDAY OF THE YEAR OR NEW YEAR'S EVE

THE eyes of the Lord are always upon you, from the beginning of the year even unto the end.

The Lord is good unto them that wait for Him, to the soul that seeketh Him.

Let us search and try our ways, and turn again to the Lord.

I

ALMIGHTY and Eternal God, with whom one day is as a thousand years, and a thousand years as one day; in whom our fathers trusted, and whose loving kindness never failed them; we, their children, believing that Thou art for ever the same, seek the peace of those whose minds are stayed on Thee. Give us grace, as we remember the way by which Thou hast led us, to offer unto Thee the worship of adoring hearts, and to rest our hopes for the time to come on Thine unchanging love; through Jesus Christ our Lord. AMEN.

O GOD, our Creator and our Judge, we would not hide our transgressions from Thee, though they be more than we can number. We confess vows unfulfilled, good purposes forgotten, opportunities neglected, duties left undone. We have spoken unkind words and done ungenerous deeds: we have cherished unholy desires, and, living for things that perish, have neglected Thee in whom is our life and peace. We have no refuge but in Thy long-suffering mercy. Show us Thy compassion; forgive, correct and heal us; through Jesus Christ our Lord. AMEN.

O LORD Jesus Christ, who didst come as at this time to renew the hopes of sinful men, and didst humble Thyself to be made like us in our weakness and need, that we might be exalted into true sonship of the Father; let the same mind be in us which was also in Thee. Help us to follow the example of Thy meekness and humility, that we may forgive others as Thou hast forgiven us. Help us to cast away every doubt and fear, and to face the uncertain future in the peace which comes from trust in Thee. And unto Thee, O Lord, with the eternal Father and the Holy Spirit, be glory for ever and ever. AMEN.

II

A LMIGHTY God, Everlasting Father, as another year draws to its close, we thank Thee for the protection, comfort and guidance Thou hast given us throughout its course.

We thank Thee for Thy goodness that hath created us, for Thy bounty that hath sustained us, for Thy fatherly discipline that hath corrected us, for Thy patience that hath borne with us. Above all, we thank Thee for Thine incarnate Son, sent as at this time to be our Saviour. Bless the Lord, O my soul, and all that is within me, bless His holy Name; through Jesus Christ our Lord. AMEN.

H EAR us, O God, we beseech Thee, as we bring the whole world of men into the fellowship of our prayers.

Build up Thy Church in strength, that the good tidings of great joy which shall be to all peoples may be spread far and wide.

We pray for all nations, that in the coming year they may be drawn into closer bonds of mutual honour and service. Let men everywhere hear Thy voice and know Thy will, that they may turn from all selfish aims and warlike deeds, and lay the government upon His shoulder who is the Prince of Peace.

We pray for our beloved land, and Empire, and for our Queen and all the Royal House, that Thy favour may rest and abide upon them. And for the Queen's counsellors and all in authority over us we beseech Thee, that Thou wilt direct their counsels and endeavours to the good government of the people, and the advancement of the peace and unity of the world.

Bless, we pray Thee, this congregation and parish, its homes and families, its schools and all its work. Fill our homes with Thy presence, and our hearts with Thy love. Watch over our dear ones who are absent from us; make their memories of home a joy and a safeguard to them, and keep them steadfast in their fidelity to Thee.

Remember in mercy those who end the year under any shadow of affliction: the lonely, the disappointed, the sick, the mourners and those whose strength faileth; give them comfort and peace, in Jesus Christ their Saviour. AMEN.

LORD of all worlds, before whom stand the living and the departed; we remember before Thee with thanksgiving those who have passed within the veil, especially those dear to us whom in the year now ending Thou hast called home to their rest.

Grant that even here we may have true communion of spirit with them; and help us so to live by faith in Thy blessed Son, that we at the last may be gathered with them, beyond the changes and chances of this fleeting world, into the Kingdom of Thy glory; through Jesus Christ our Lord, who liveth and reigneth, and is worshipped and glorified with Thee and the Holy Spirit, world without end. AMEN.

III

O LORD of love and truth; enrich our hearts with Thy love and cause the light of truth to shine forth for us as we hearken to Thy word; give us grace to follow whithersoever it may lead us, that we may keep the way of righteousness even unto the end; through Jesus Christ our Lord. AMEN.

IV

O GOD, who amidst life's changes abidest ever the same, Eternal Love, Eternal Truth, Eternal Life; enable us to know the greatness of the trust committed to our keeping in this life; and grant that, learning aright the lessons of the past, we may henceforth walk in wisdom, love Thee unto death, and finally awaken to serve Thee with a perfect heart in the joy of the life eternal; through Jesus Christ our Lord, who liveth and reigneth, and is worshipped and glorified, with Thee and the Holy Spirit, world without end. AMEN.

SERVICE FOR NEW YEAR'S DAY
OR FOR THE FIRST
SUNDAY OF THE YEAR

If the first Sunday of the year is also the Sunday of the Epiphany (Jan. 6), use may be made of the service for the Epiphany.

LORD, thou hast been our dwelling-place in all generations. Fear not, for I am with thee, saith the Lord: be not dismayed, for I am thy God.

I

ETERNAL God who hast been our dwelling-place in all generations, and hast compassed our days with blessing; we praise and adore Thy glorious name, and give thanks unto Thee for Thine unchanging goodness. At the beginning of another year we Thy children, whose times are in Thy hand, cast ourselves anew upon Thy mercy, and commit ourselves to Thy fatherly care; who livest and reignest, Father, Son, and Holy Spirit, one God, for evermore. AMEN.

O GOD, who knowest the secrets of our hearts; we humbly confess before Thee our many sins and shortcomings, especially those by which we have grieved Thee in the year now past. We have not kept the vows we made at its beginning; we have yielded to temptation and have ofttimes forgotten Thee.

Most merciful God, who hast not dealt with us after our sins, nor rewarded us according to our iniquities: we beseech Thee to forgive us. Make us glad according to the days wherein Thou hast afflicted us, and the years wherein we have seen evil. Incline our hearts henceforward to keep Thy commandments, and make us partakers of Thine eternal kingdom; through Jesus Christ our Lord. AMEN.

ALMIGHTY Father, we pray Thee graciously to lead us through the uncertainties of this new year of our earthly pilgrimage. Protect us from the dangers of the way; prepare us for the duties, the trials, the joys and sorrows that await us; and grant that each change the year brings with it may bring us nearer to Thyself, and to the eternal joy and rest that await the faithful in Thy blessed and glorious presence; through Jesus Christ our Lord. AMEN.

O SAVIOUR of the world, who as at this time wast named Jesus, according to the word of the angel; fulfil unto us, we beseech Thee, the gracious promise of that holy name. Of Thy great mercy save Thy people from their sins; and grant that, as they have joy and peace in Thy name, they may labour abundantly to publish it unto all nations; who livest and reignest with the Father, and with the Holy Spirit, one God, world without end. AMEN.

II

O GOD, who hast commanded us in everything to give thanks; we praise Thy name for all Thy goodness and mercy unto us. For the way by which Thou hast led us and the gifts Thou hast bestowed, for the joys Thou madest to abound to us and for the sorrows and trials Thou didst overrule for good, we give Thee thanks. For the measure of success Thou hast granted to our labours, and the sure guidance Thou hast given in every path of duty, we praise Thee. And chiefly at this season we magnify Thy holy name for Thy best and greatest gift in Jesus Christ Thy Son our Lord, the same yesterday, today and forever. Grant that we show forth Thy praise by walking in His ways all the days of our life; for His name's sake, to whom with Thee and the Holy Spirit, one God, be all honour and praise, world without end. AMEN.

ALMIGHTY God, we pray for Thy holy Church throughout the world. Revive Thy work in the midst of the years and grant to Thy people everywhere a new zeal for Thee. Let Thy Church be alert in Thy service and quick to seize whatever opportunity the coming days may bring to witness for Thee and to labour for Thy kingdom.

Almighty God, whose blessed Son was circumcised as at this time in fulfilment of the covenant made with Abraham, and in token of His membership of the Jewish race, we pray for Thine ancient people, that Thou wouldest take away the veil from their hearts, and bring them into the fold of Thy holy Church.

We pray for our nation and Empire. Teach us in all our ways to acknowledge Thee, and do Thou direct our paths. Bless the Queen and the Royal Family. Grant that they may be sustained by the love and loyalty of the people and find rest and strength in Thee. Surround the throne with faithful and wise counsellors, and grant to the whole body of the people such increase of understanding, sympathy, and brotherly kindness, that peace and concord may ever abide among them.

Almighty God, the comfort of the sad and the

strength of them that suffer; let the prayers of Thy children who cry out of any tribulation come unto Thee, that all may rejoice to know that Thy mercy is present with them in their affliction. Succour the oppressed and down-trodden, the poor, and them that have no helper. Heal the sick, comfort those who mourn, and give such faith to all who suffer that through their affliction Thou mayest set forward Thy purposes of love.

We pray for our friends and kinsfolk wherever they be; shield them from danger, provide them with the means of grace, keep them pure in their lives and steadfast in their ways, and teach us all to know that Thou art ever near, and that they and we are one for ever in Thee.

We remember, O Lord, all who have died confessing the holy name of Jesus, especially those whom Thou hast taken to Thyself during the past year, and those ever dear to ourselves. Grant that at the last we, with them, may be found in the company of those who are sealed with that name; through the same Jesus Christ our Lord, who liveth and reigneth with Thee and the Holy Ghost, God blessed for ever. AMEN.

III

O GOD, whose word is quick and powerful, and sharper than any two-edged sword; grant unto us who are here before Thee that we may receive Thy truth into our hearts, in faith and love. By it may we be taught and guided, upheld and comforted; that being no longer children in understanding, we may be prepared unto every good work and grow to the stature of the fullness of Christ. AMEN.

IV

O GOD, who art from everlasting to everlasting, and hast vouchsafed to us a new beginning of days; grant us, we pray Thee, throughout this year, such prosperity as Thou seest to be good for us, and make us to abound in such works as are pleasing unto Thee. As days and years pass over us, teach us to be more thankful for past mercies, more penitent for past faults, and more earnest to serve Thee in the years that Thou shalt give us, that so we may look forward with increasing joy to the new year of eternal life; through Jesus Christ our Lord. AMEN.

EPIPHANY

THE MANIFESTATION OF CHRIST
TO THE GENTILES

*If the Sunday of the Epiphany is also the first Sunday
of the Year, use may be made of the Service for the
First Sunday of the Year.*

FROM the rising of the sun unto the going down
of the same My Name shall be great among the
Gentiles, saith the Lord of hosts, and in every
place incense shall be offered unto My name and a
pure offering.

Arise, shine; for thy light is come, and the glory
of the Lord is risen upon thee.

Jesus said, I am the Light of the world: he that
followeth Me shall not walk in darkness, but shall
have the light of life.

I

O GOD, who art from everlasting to everlasting, Creator and Upholder of all things, Source
of all life and light; we worship and adore Thee.
Great art Thou, and greatly to be praised; Thy
greatness is unsearchable. Look mercifully upon
us, we beseech Thee, and shew us Thy glory. Let
the light of Thy love arise and shine upon us, that
the darkness of our souls may vanish before the
beams of Thy brightness; and blessed be Thy
name, O Father, Son, and Holy Spirit, from this
time forth, and for evermore. AMEN.

GOD of all mercy and grace, who knowest the thoughts and desires of our hearts, and art acquainted with all our ways; stir us to shame and true contrition for the shortcomings and sins which in Thy presence rise up in judgement against us. We confess that, although Thou hast given us light, we have often turned aside into darkness; our eyes have not been open to Thy glory, nor have our minds freely received Thy truth. Walking in carelessness, we have fallen into much error, and have failed to guide others into the way of life and joy. Forgive, we beseech Thee, our failures in faith and loyalty, our unworthiness and sin.

Almighty and most merciful God, who desirest not the death of a sinner; mercifully grant to us absolution of our sins, and in the days to come give us grace to serve Thee more faithfully; through Jesus Christ our Saviour. AMEN.

O GOD, who didst guide the wise men to behold Thy Son our Lord; show us Thy heavenly light, and give us grace to follow until we find Him, and, finding Him, rejoice. And grant that, as they presented gold, frankincense, and myrrh, we now may bring Him the offering of a loving heart, an adoring spirit, and an obedient will, for His honour, and for Thy glory, O God Most High. AMEN.

O LORD Jesus Christ, Son of the Highest, who didst come to give light to all that are in darkness; fill us with Thine own infinite love to men; and since Thou hast entrusted to us the knowledge of Thy truth and the gifts of Thy bounty, help us to use them as good stewards, that we may share in bringing all men to Thy light and hastening the

coming of Thy kingdom; who with the Father, in
the unity of the Spirit, livest and reignest, God for
ever and ever. AMEN.

II

ALMIGHTY and Eternal God, Maker of all
things visible and invisible; we bless Thee
that Thou hast not hidden Thyself from them that
truly seek Thee. Heaven and earth are full of Thy
glory, and all Thy works proclaim Thy power. We
bless Thee that Thou dost rule and govern the
world which Thou hast made: day by day Thou
dost sustain it, and for the good of Thy children
bringest forth out of Thy treasures things new and
old. We bless Thee that Thou hast never left Thy
children without guidance, but hast written Thy
law in their hearts; by Thy prophets Thou hast
spoken; and by Thy Son, Christ Jesus, whom
Thou gavest to be the Light of the world, Thou
hast made plain the way of life. For these so great
mercies and for all Thy loving kindness and Thy
truth, we praise Thee, O God; through Jesus
Christ our Lord. AMEN.

ALMIGHTY God, the brightness of faithful
souls, who didst bring the Gentiles to Thy
light through Him who is the bright and morning
Star; fill the world speedily, we beseech Thee, with
Thy glory, and show Thyself to all nations. Send
forth Thy light and truth into the dark places of
the earth. Dispel the night of error and fear, and
upon all who wait for Thy light let the Sun of
Righteousness arise.
   O Lord, who lovest the Church which is Thy
witness to the world; cleanse and sanctify her more

and more by Thy Spirit, that the flame of true faith may burn in her with ever increasing brightness, bringing those who walk in darkness to Thy light.

O God, who makest men to be Thy messengers; bestow Thy Spirit of grace and power on those who have gone forth to preach the gospel in distant lands. Uphold them in discouragement, protect them in danger, strengthen them to overcome all hindrances; and by their labour and sacrifice let the good tidings of great joy be carried speedily into all the world. Build up the young Churches in faith and strength, and by their living witness let many souls be gathered into Thy kingdom.

Hear us, O Lord, as we ask for our country Thy continued favour and help. Give wisdom and guidance to our Queen and her counsellors. Teach us, as a people, to seek first Thy righteousness, and add to us all things needful for our welfare. Increase evermore among us good will and concord, justice and charity.

O Lord our God, whose blessed Son has promised that those who follow Him shall not walk in darkness but shall have the light of life; have pity upon all who are afflicted by doubt or perplexity, and grant that they may see Thy light in Jesus, and learn, amid the mysteries of life, to walk humbly by faith in Him.

Merciful Father, whose compassions are infinite; hear us as we pray Thee to relieve the pains of those who suffer, and to assuage the griefs of the sorrowing and the bereaved. Through the dark shadows of their affliction let them see the clear shining of Thy love, and cheer them with the promise of life everlasting; through Jesus Christ our Lord. AMEN.

ALMIGHTY God, with whom do rest the spirits of them that depart hence in the Lord; receive our thanksgiving for all the faithful who now rest in peace with Thee, and especially for those whom we have loved on earth. Keep our love for them unwasted and unchanged, and sustain us in communion of spirit with them, till they and we are united again for ever, in the light and joy of Thy heaven; through Jesus Christ our Lord, who liveth and reigneth with Thee and the Holy Spirit, one God, world without end. AMEN.

III

O GOD, who hast given us Thy holy word, that we may learn Thy truth and know Thy will; give light to our understanding, we beseech Thee, that we may rightly perceive and know what Thou wouldst have us to be and do; and endue us with grace and power ever to follow Thee; through Jesus Christ our Lord. AMEN.

IV

O GOD who by the leading of a star didst manifest Thy only begotten Son to the Gentiles; mercifully grant that we, who know Thee now by faith, may after this life be brought to contemplate the beauty of Thy majesty; through Jesus Christ our Lord. AMEN.

FIRST SUNDAY IN LENT

REND your heart, and not your garments, and turn unto the Lord your God: for He is gracious and merciful, slow to anger and of great kindness.

Jesus said, If any man will come after Me, let him deny himself, and take up his cross, and follow Me.

I

O LORD our God, long-suffering and full of compassion; be present with us now, we beseech Thee, as we come before Thee with our sorrows and our sins, to ask for Thy comfort and forgiveness. We thank Thee for this season of thought and prayer in which we make ready to recall our Saviour's sufferings and to celebrate His triumph. Grant us the aid of Thy Holy Spirit, that as we acknowledge our sins and implore Thy pardon, we may also be enabled to deny ourselves, and be upheld in the hour of temptation; through Jesus Christ our Lord. AMEN.

O LORD our God, who art of purer eyes than to behold iniquity; have mercy upon us, we beseech Thee, for our sins accuse us, and we are troubled by them and put to shame. We have done wrong to ourselves in ignorance, and to our brethren in wilfulness, and by our selfish and faithless ways have grieved Thy Holy Spirit. Forgive us, we humbly pray; through Jesus Christ our Lord. AMEN.

ALMIGHTY and everlasting God, who hatest nothing that Thou hast made, and dost forgive the sins of all them that are penitent; create and make in us new and contrite hearts, that we, worthily lamenting our sins and acknowledging our wretchedness, may obtain of Thee, the God of all mercy, perfect remission and forgiveness; through Jesus Christ our Lord. AMEN.

O GOD, who didst suffer Thine only Son to be tempted, that He might be able to succour them that are tempted; we beseech Thee to save us from those snares and temptations by which we are continually beset, and so strengthen us by Thy good Spirit that in all things we may be more than conquerors; through Him that loved us and washed us from our sins in His own blood, even Jesus Christ our Lord. AMEN.

ALMIGHTY God, whose blessed Son Jesus Christ was made perfect through the things which He suffered; mercifully enable us, His disciples, to meet the toils and sufferings of our daily life with faith and patience; and make us wise by tribulation, and strong to bear our cross; through the same Jesus Christ our Lord. AMEN.

O HEAVENLY Father, whose blessed Son has taught us that whosoever will be His disciple must take up his cross and follow Him; help us with willing heart to mortify our sinful affections, and depart from every selfish indulgence by which we sin against Thee. Strengthen us to resist temptation, and to walk in the narrow way that leadeth unto life; through Jesus Christ our Lord, to whom, with Thee and the Holy Ghost, one God, be all glory and honour, world without end. AMEN.

II

O LORD our God, whose name is great and whose goodness is inexhaustible; Thou art worthy to receive blessing and thanksgiving at all times from all Thy people, for Thy mercy endureth for ever.

WE praise Thy name for the loving kindness Thou hast manifested to us, in the unfailing blessings of Thy bountiful providence, and in the keeping and guidance that have brought us to this hour. For those tokens of Thy goodness which are specially present this day to our thankful remembrance we praise Thee. But most of all we glorify Thee for revealing Thyself in Jesus Christ. We bless Thee that He was in all points tempted like as we are, yet without sin. We thank Thee for the Cross that He carried, and for the death that He died. We praise Thee for His victory over death and the grave, and for the hope we have in Him of life eternal; who liveth and reigneth with Thee and the Holy Spirit, one God, world without end. AMEN.

ALMIGHTY God, who hast founded Thy Church to be Thy dwelling place for ever; cleanse it, we pray Thee, from everything that offends Thee; beautify the place of Thy sanctuary, and make it an eternal excellency.

Continue Thy favour, we beseech Thee, to the Church of our own land. Strengthen its faith, increase its zeal, and revive its work. Cheer and inspire the faithful; cause those who forget or deny Thee to remember and return; and let Thy power and glory be seen in Thy house as in the days of old.

We pray for all nations, that as Thou hast given them to Thy Son for His inheritance they may by the increasing power of His Cross become His sure possession, and be drawn ever closer unto Him who, being lifted up, reigneth over all men from the Tree.

We pray for our own nation and the empire Thou hast committed to our trust. Continue Thy favour to our Queen. Keep her firm in fidelity to Thee, that her life and reign may long continue to be a blessing to her people. Give wisdom to our leaders, that, ruling in equity, they may preserve liberty and tranquillity throughout our borders. Let wisdom and knowledge be the stability of our times, and fear of Thee be our strong confidence for ever.

Almighty God, who makest the sun to rise on the evil and the good, and sendest rain on the just and on the unjust; we beseech Thee at this season to regard with Thy favour those who till the soil, and to send Thine abundant blessing on the earth; that it may bring forth its fruits in due season, and that we, being filled with Thy bounty, may evermore give thanks unto Thee, the Giver of all good.

We pray for thy suffering children. Be thou the Friend of the friendless, the Support of the poor, the Healer of the sick, the Light and Life of the dying.

We pray for our loved ones wheresoever they be, whether at home with us or in homes of their own, in our cities, upon the sea, or in far-off lands. Let Thy presence with them be their shield and stay. Forbid, O God, that our beloved should ever have cause to be ashamed of us, or we of them; through Jesus Christ our Lord. AMEN.

O GOD, in whose hand are the souls of the righteous; we praise Thy holy Name for all Thy
servants who have finished their course in Thy
faith and fear, and are now at rest with Thee; and
we pray that, encouraged by their example and
strengthened by their fellowship, we may so pass
through things temporal that we fail not to attain
with them to things eternal; through Jesus Christ
our Lord, to whom, with Thee the Father and
the Holy Spirit, be all glory now and evermore.
AMEN.

III

O GOD, who by Thy Word and Spirit dost
marvellously work out the reconciliation of
mankind; enlighten our minds in the knowledge of
Thy Son, that we may continue in the fellowship
of Thy children, and obtain Thy promises which
exceed all we can desire; through the same Jesus
Christ our Lord. AMEN.

IV

O GOD, whose only begotten Son followed the
way of faith and duty even to the crown of
thorns and the Cross; give us grace that we may
learn the harder lessons of our faith; and so endue
us with power from on high, that, taking up our
cross and following our Saviour in His patience
and humility, we may enter into the fellowship of
His sufferings, and come at last to dwell with Him
in His eternal kingdom; through the same Jesus
Christ our Lord. AMEN.

SECOND SUNDAY IN LENT

GOD is a Spirit; and they that worship Him must worship Him in spirit and in truth.

A broken and a contrite heart, O God, Thou wilt not despise.

I

O GOD, eternal and ever blessed, who callest us to worship Thee in spirit and in truth; look mercifully upon us as we worship and adore Thee. Order what is disordered in our lives, bring our minds to Thy truth, our conscience to Thy law, and our hearts to Thy love; that, in fellowship with all Thy Church, we may hear Thy voice and be enabled to answer Thee with humble trust and willing obedience; through Jesus Christ our Lord. AMEN.

ALMIGHTY God, spirit of peace and of grace, whose salvation is never far from penitent hearts; we confess the sins that have estranged us from Thee, dimmed our vision of heavenly things, and brought upon us many troubles and sorrows. We remember with shame how often we have forgotten our duties and lost our faith.

O merciful Father, grant unto us who humble ourselves before Thee, the remission of all our sins and the assurance of Thy pardon and peace; through Jesus Christ our Lord. AMEN.

GRANT, O God, that we may be ready to respond to the voice of Thy indwelling spirit; that we may live in loving obedience to Thee and in charity with all men. Help us to forgive as we would be forgiven, dwelling neither in speech nor in thought upon offences committed against us, but seeking to overcome evil with good. And, as the Son of Man came not to be ministered unto but to minister, make us willing to spend and to be spent in Thy service; that we may finish the work Thou gavest us to do, and finally by Thy mercy, be numbered with those who behold Thy face in glory; through the same Jesus Christ our Lord. AMEN.

ALMIGHTY God, who seest that we have no power of ourselves to help ourselves; keep us both outwardly in our bodies, and inwardly in our souls; that we may be defended from all adversities which may happen to the body, and from all evil thoughts which may assault and hurt the soul; through Jesus Christ our Lord. AMEN.

ALMIGHTY and everlasting God, who hatest nothing that thou hast made, and dost forgive the sins of all them that are penitent; create and make in us new and contrite hearts, that we, worthily lamenting our sins, and acknowledging our wretchedness, may obtain of Thee, the God of all mercy, perfect remission and forgiveness; through Jesus Christ our Lord, who livest and reignest with Thee and the Holy Spirit, one God, blessed for ever. AMEN.

II

O LORD our God, Creator and Upholder of all things, Source of light and life, worthy art Thou to receive glory and honour, thanksgiving and praise.

WE call to remembrance before Thee the bounties of Thy Providence, and Thy fatherly care
by which we are sustained. We thank Thee for the
dear ones and friends Thou hast given us; and for
the human sympathy through which we are brought
to know Thy Divine love. Above all we bless Thee
for the grace and truth that are in Jesus Christ, for
our redemption by His death on the Cross, and for
the presence and comfort of Thy Holy Spirit in
our hearts. With all Thy benefits, give us steadfast and obedient hearts, that we may praise Thee
in our lives by continually walking in Thy ways;
through Jesus Christ our Lord, to whom with
Thee and the Holy Spirit, be all laud, honour, and
majesty, world without end. AMEN.

ALMIGHTY God, arm, we beseech Thee, with
the sword of Thy Holy Spirit, Thy Church
universal, that it may be strong to curb every
opposition, to make arrogance dumb before Thee,
and to lighten the dark places of our guilt and woe.

Send forth labourers into the harvest; defend
them in danger and temptation; and gird them
with Thy truth; that the way of the Lord be prepared throughout the whole earth, and those who
sit in darkness and in the shadow of death, be
brought into Thy marvellous light.

O God, in whose favour alone are the happiness
and well-being of a nation; we pray for our country
and empire; that Thy servant Elizabeth, our Queen,
and all the Royal Family, may be enriched by Thy
grace; that a wise and steadfast spirit may prevail
in our parliaments and councils; and that all who are
set in authority over us may advance Thy kingdom,
and lead the people in the ways of righteousness.

D

O God, most gracious and most merciful, we pray for all whose need cries out to Thee: the sick in body, the sad of heart, the troubled in mind. We pray for the bereaved, and for those in whose hearts faith burns low, hope grows dim, and love turns cold. For the sake of Thy beloved Son, the man of sorrows and acquainted with grief, let Thy light arise in their darkness, Thy comfort assuage their sorrows, and Thy peace possess their hearts.

To Thy gracious keeping we commend all whom we love, wheresoever they may be. . . . Uphold them, O God, in all their ways; and grant them health of body, peace of mind, and courage of heart; through Jesus Christ our Lord. AMEN.

GLORY be to Thee, O Christ, for Thy Church which waits for Thee here, and for Thy servants who see Thee in the light that excelleth. In the fellowship of Thy Spirit and the communion of Thy saints, with the faithful and true of all ages and climes, with our own beloved who are at peace in Thy presence, we who now live and labour on earth unite in ascribing unto Thee with the Father and the Holy Spirit, thanksgiving, glory, honour, and power, for ever and ever. AMEN.

III

LET Thy Spirit, O Lord, illumine our minds and, as Thy Son hath promised, lead us into all truth; through the same our Lord Jesus Christ. AMEN.

IV

O LORD Jesus Christ, who in the days of Thy flesh didst accept those who ministered unto Thee of their substance, bless us and our offerings for Thy service. Deepen in us the gladness of devotion to Thee; and as Thou didst finish the work which Thy Father gave Thee to do, grant us not to weary in well-doing, but to go forth in Thy strength, and persevere even to the end. For Thine own name's sake we ask it. AMEN.

THIRD SUNDAY IN LENT

COME now, and let us reason together, saith the Lord; though your sins be as scarlet, they shall be white as snow; though they be red like crimson, they shall be as wool.

Let us search and try our ways, and turn again to the Lord.

I

ALMIGHTY God, who of Thy great mercy hast gathered us into Thy visible Church; grant that we may not swerve from the purity of Thy worship, but may so honour Thee both in spirit and in outward form that Thy name may be glorified in us, and that our fellowship may be with all Thy saints in earth and in heaven; through Jesus Christ our Lord. AMEN.

ALMIGHTY God we confess unto Thee that we have sinned exceedingly in thought, word and deed. We have neglected opportunities of good: we have sought the things which are temporal and have forgotten the things which are eternal. Wherefore we beseech Thee to have mercy upon us.

Almighty and everlasting God, who hatest nothing that Thou hast made, and dost forgive the sins of all them that are penitent; create and make in us new and contrite hearts, that we, worthily lamenting our sins, and acknowledging our wretchedness, may obtain of Thee, the God of all mercy, perfect remission and forgiveness; through Jesus Christ our Lord. AMEN.

FROM the lust of the flesh, the lust of the eyes, and the pride of life, good Lord, deliver us. Strengthen us by the power of the Holy Spirit, to fight the good fight of faith, to endure hardness as good soldiers of Jesus Christ, to rule our bodies by temperance and our spirits by meekness, and to glorify Thee alike with our bodies and our spirits, which are Thine.

Unite us in a true and living faith with Jesus Christ our Saviour: suffering with Him here, may we reign with Him hereafter, and bearing now His Cross may we hereafter wear His crown.

We beseech Thee, Almighty God, look upon the hearty desires of Thy humble servants, and stretch forth the right hand of Thy majesty, to be our defence against all our enemies; through Jesus Christ our Lord. AMEN.

ALMIGHTY God, whose blessed Son was tempted that He might be able to succour and help all them that are tempted; we beseech Thee to save us from those snares and temptations by which we are continually beset, and so to strengthen us mightily by Thy good Spirit that in all things we may be more than conquerors; through Him who loved us and bore our sins upon the tree, even Jesus Christ our Lord. AMEN.

II

ALMIGHTY God, the fountain of all goodness, we Thy children call to remembrance Thy mercies, and we bless and praise Thy holy name. For all the blessings of this life we thank Thee, but above all we praise Thee for Jesus Christ our Saviour. That He took upon Him the form of a

servant, and the likeness of sinful flesh, and fulfilled Thy law, and was obedient even unto death,
we praise Thee; that He made propitiation for our
sins, and that when He had overcome the sharpness
of death, He opened the kingdom of heaven to
all believers, we praise Thee; that He ever liveth
to make intercession, and saveth to the uttermost them that come to Thee by Him, we praise
Thee; and we glorify Thy name for ever and ever.
AMEN.

ALMIGHTY God our heavenly Father, we beseech Thee to receive the humble intercessions which, through the merits and mediation of
Thy Son, we offer unto Thee.

We pray for Thy holy Church universal, that all
who profess Thy name may be careful to maintain
good works; that the weak may be strengthened,
the wanderers restored, the sorrowful comforted
and the doubting confirmed.

O God, King of kings, and Lord of lords,
remember all to whom Thou hast given authority
upon earth. Especially we beseech Thee to look
with favour upon our Sovereign Lady Queen
Elizabeth, Elizabeth the Queen Mother, Philip,
Duke of Edinburgh, Charles, Prince of Wales,
and all the Royal House.

Endue with Thy heavenly wisdom the Queen's
ministers, the High Court of Parliament, and all
who direct the affairs of this nation and empire.

We pray for the Queen's forces by sea and land
and air: protect them from all evil and make them
strong to defend the right.

Look mercifully upon all in trouble, whether of
body, mind or estate. Sustain and heal the sick;

support and sanctify the dying; visit with Thy mercy all who mourn.

We bless Thy name for all who have died in the Lord, who rest from their labours and whose works do follow them. Grant that we, walking like them in Thy faith and fear, may with them be made partakers of Thy heavenly kingdom; through Jesus Christ our Lord, to whom with Thee and the Holy Spirit, be all honour and glory, world without end. AMEN.

III

O GOD, who guidest the meek in judgment and teachest them Thy way; we beseech Thee to give unto us Thy Holy Spirit and the wisdom that cometh from above: grant that Thy word may have free course and be glorified; may we receive it with joy and thankfulness, and be strengthened and purified thereby; so that with steadfast faith we may serve Thee, and abide to our life's end in Thy love and fear: through Jesus Christ our Lord. AMEN.

IV

O GOD our Father, we beseech Thee to accept our worship. Pardon its imperfections; and grant that henceforth, enlightened by the teaching, guided by the example, and sanctified by the Spirit of Thy well beloved Son, we may walk in newness of life, and so prepare for that blessedness which Thou hast promised to Thy children in heaven; through Jesus Christ our Lord. AMEN.

FOURTH SUNDAY IN LENT

LIFT up your eyes, for your redemption draweth nigh.

The darkness is passing away, and the true light already shineth.

Rejoice ye with Jerusalem and be glad with her, all ye that love her.

I was glad when they said unto me, Let us go into the house of the Lord.

I

O LORD our father, whose thoughts towards us are thoughts of good and not of evil, who hast spared us and protected us, and hast brought us to this hour; we come into Thy house in the multitude of Thy mercies, and we praise and bless Thy holy name.

O Lord Jesus Christ our Saviour, who broughtest hearing to the deaf, sight to the blind, and life to the dead, who, for us men and for our salvation, didst suffer at men's hands and didst die upon the Cross of Calvary; we rejoice in the redemption which Thou hast purchased for us.

O Holy Spirit, Lord and Giver of life, bring to our minds the things that are Christ's, that we may live anew in the light of His love.

Grant, we beseech Thee, Almighty God, that we who know our weakness and trust in Thy mercy, may ever rejoice in Thy loving-kindness; Father, Son, and Holy Spirit, Blessed Trinity, to whom be glory, wisdom, and power, world without end. AMEN.

ALMIGHTY God, we confess ourselves un-worthy of the least of Thy mercies. Thou hast made us for Thyself, but we have gone our own ways and done our own pleasure. We have not loved Thee with all our heart and with all our soul, with all our strength and with all our mind. We have been intent on our own advancement, and have passed our neighbour by on the other side.

Lover of the souls of men, forgive us, so that we, who for our evil deeds do worthily deserve to be punished, by the comfort of Thy grace may mercifully be relieved; through our Lord and Saviour Jesus Christ. AMEN.

MAY Thy grace turn us from our unworthy ways to walk in the ways of Thy love; that enduring hardness as good soldiers of Jesus Christ we may deny ourselves and take up our Cross and follow Him. So may we be kind one to another, tender-hearted, forgiving one another, even as Thou in Christ hast forgiven us. And to Thee shall be praise and glory for ever. AMEN.

II

O LORD our God, who hast so wonderfully made man, and more wonderfully hast re-deemed him, we praise and bless Thy holy name for all the wonder of Thy love. For the life Thou givest us, with its opportunities of service and sacrifice, and for all earthly blessings, we give Thee thanks. For the example of those who have tended and guided us, for those who have taught us to look to Thee and led us on our heavenward journey, we bless and praise Thy holy name. But above all we praise Thee for Thy mercy declared unto mankind in Christ Jesus our Lord; for the record of His life and His passion and His Cross, for the light immortal that shines from Him upon the darkest places, and for the hope that He has brought of an inheritance incorruptible and undefiled, and that fadeth not away. Help us to accept Thy mercies in humble thankfulness, and ever to walk in the way of Thy commandments; through the same Jesus Christ our Lord. AMEN.

HEAR us as we pray for the whole family of mankind. Hasten the coming of Thy kingdom, when from the rising of the sun to the going down of the same all men shall be glad in Thee. Bring together all nations in the knowledge of Thy love and in common service, till the kingdoms of this world become the kingdom of our Lord and of His Christ.

Grant to Thy Church a surer hold on faith, hope and charity, that she may ever learn new things out of Thy word, seek more earnestly to follow Thy leading, and declare Thy will without fear.

We pray for our country, for our Queen and her ministers, and for all sorts and conditions of men in her realm. Inspire and uphold those on whom the trust of their fellows has laid burdens, that they may be guided by the wisdom which is from above.

Heavenly Father, after whom all parenthood in heaven and earth is named; bless we beseech Thee all children, and give to their parents Thy spirit of wisdom; that the homes in which they grow up may be to them an image of Thy kingdom, and the love of their parents a likeness of Thy love.

O Almighty God, who hast created the earth for man, and man for Thy glory; mercifully hear the supplications of Thy people, and be mindful of Thy covenant; that the earth may yield her increase;

and the good seed bring forth abundantly, to the glory of Thy holy name.

Have mercy upon all who walk in carelessness or sin, unheeding of Thy love. Lift up the fallen, restore the wandering, and on the disquieted bestow Thy peace. Grant to the sick and the suffering, and to all who are laden with care and tribulation, the refreshment of Thy presence. Comfort those who mourn their dead, and raise their thoughts to that world where they dwell with Thee.

Finally we beseech Thee to hear us as we remember with thanksgiving all who have lived in Thy faith and fear and serve Thee now in glory everlasting. Help us to follow them as they followed Christ, and when our warfare on earth is over, and our labour done, grant that we may meet with them in Thine everlasting kingdom. And to Thee, O God, Father, Son, and Holy Spirit, be all glory and honour and power, now and for ever. AMEN.

III

GRANT we beseech Thee, Almighty God, that Thy grace may make fruitful to us our meditations on the sacrifice of our Redeemer; that as earthly things grow dim, things heavenly may grow more clear; through Jesus Christ our Lord. AMEN.

IV

O LORD God, merciful and gracious, long-suffering and abundant in goodness and truth; enter not into judgment with Thy servants, we beseech Thee, but be pleased of Thy kindness to grant that we, who are justly afflicted and bowed down with the sense of our sins, may be refreshed and lifted up with the joy of Thy salvation; through Jesus Christ our Lord. AMEN.

FIFTH SUNDAY IN LENT
PASSION SUNDAY

GOD commendeth His love towards us, in that, while we were yet sinners, Christ died for us. He suffered for us, leaving us an example, that we should follow in His steps.

I

ALMIGHTY God, Eternal Father, who didst not spare Thine own Son, but didst deliver Him up for us all; in humility and penitence we draw nigh unto Thee. As we call to remembrance the passion and sufferings of Thy holy Son, we beseech Thee to stir up within us the precious gift of faith; that we may rejoice in Thy great salvation, and offer unto Thee the worship of our hearts and the obedience of our lives; through the same Jesus Christ our Lord. AMEN.

O GOD, most holy and most merciful, we humbly confess in Thy presence that we have sinned against Thee. We have wandered from Thy paths; we have been unfaithful in the trust committed to us; we have failed in faith, in hope, and in charity. By our blindness and selfishness, our lack of brotherly love, and our distrust of Thy gracious promises, we have grieved Thy holy Spirit. Our only hope is in Thy mercy. Reveal unto us our need of Thy cleansing and redeeming power, and bring us to a true repentance.

Almighty and everlasting God, who hatest nothing that Thou hast made, and dost forgive the sins of all them that are penitent; create and make in us new and contrite hearts, that we worthily lamenting our sins, and acknowledging our wretchedness, may obtain of Thee, the God of all mercy, perfect remission and forgiveness; through Jesus Christ our Lord. AMEN.

O GOD, who by the Cross and passion of Thy Son Jesus Christ didst save and deliver mankind; grant that by steadfast faith in the merits of that holy sacrifice we may find help and salvation, and may triumph in the power of His victory; through the same Jesus Christ our Lord. AMEN.

O GOD, whose blessed Son did suffer for all mankind; grant unto us that, rightly observing this holy season, we may learn to know Thee better, to love Thee more, and to serve Thee with a more perfect will; through the same Jesus Christ our Lord, who liveth and reigneth, and is worshipped and glorified, with Thee and the Holy Spirit, one God, world without end. AMEN.

II

ALMIGHTY and most merciful God, we lift up our hearts to Thee with thanksgiving and praise for Thy loving-kindness and tender mercies towards us Thy children. For our creation, preservation, and redemption; for the peace and joy of forgiveness, and for the promise of eternal life in Jesus Christ, we praise Thy name. We bless Thee that He came to do Thy holy will, to finish the work Thou gavest Him to do, and to endure suffering and affliction, even to the pain and anguish of the Cross, that we might be saved from our sins, and know the joy of Thy redeeming love.

Give us grace, with thankful hearts, to present ourselves a living sacrifice, holy and acceptable unto
Thee, which is our reasonable service; through the
same Jesus Christ our Lord. AMEN.

ALMIGHTY God, Lord of heaven and earth,
who hast promised to reveal Thy glory among
all nations; receive the solemn intercessions which
we offer in the name of our great High Priest and
Redeemer.

Remember for good Thy Church throughout the
world, and establish her in the ways of righteousness, truth, and obedience to Thy holy will. Bless
Thy people everywhere, and accept the devotion of
their hearts and the labours of their hands.

O God, the Physician of men and nations, the
Restorer of the years that have been destroyed;
look upon our distracted world, and be pleased to
complete the work of Thy healing hand. Draw all
men unto Thee and one to another by the bands of
Thy love; make Thy Church one, and fill it with
Thy Spirit, that by Thy power it may unite the
world in a sacred brotherhood of nations, wherein
justice, mercy, faith, truth and freedom may
flourish, and Thou mayest ever be glorified.

Almighty God, who rulest over all, we pray for
this realm and empire. Keep us as a people ever
mindful of our great inheritance, and strengthen us
in the resolve to serve Thee with all our powers, to
the glory of Thy holy name. Grant wisdom to the
Queen and to all in authority over us, that truth and
justice, happiness and peace, may be established
amongst us.

O Almighty Father, who through Thy Son Jesus
Christ hast consecrated labour to the blessing of

mankind; prosper, we pray Thee, the industries of this land; defend those who are engaged therein from all perils, and grant that they may rejoice in the fruits of Thy bounty, and bless Thee for Thy loving-kindness.

O God, our heavenly Father, we commend unto Thy loving care all who are joined to us by the ties of kindred, friendship and love. Keep them, we beseech Thee, both outwardly in their bodies and inwardly in their souls, and let Thy merciful blessing ever rest upon them.

O God, whose presence is everywhere, and whose mercy never faileth; graciously regard all who are in trouble or danger, and especially those known to ourselves, whom we name in our hearts before Thee. Guide the perplexed, defend the wronged, restore the lost, heal the sick, befriend the lonely, comfort the sorrowing, and receive the dying to Thy rest; through Jesus Christ our Lord. AMEN.

ETERNAL Lord God, who holdest all souls in life; shed forth, we beseech Thee, on Thy whole Church in heaven and on earth the bright beams of Thy light and heavenly comfort. Receive our thanksgiving for those who have loved and served Thee here and are now at rest with Thee; and grant that we, following their good example, may at the last enter with them into the fullness of Thine unending joy; through Jesus Christ our Lord, to whom, with Thee and the Holy Spirit, one God, be glory and praise, world without end. AMEN.

III

O GOD, who didst speak in times past unto the fathers by the prophets, and hast in these last days spoken to us by Thy Son; give us, we pray

Thee, humble, teachable, and obedient hearts, that we may receive what He hath revealed, and do always what He hath commanded. And as man liveth not by bread alone, but by every word of God; grant that we may ever hunger after this heavenly food, and find in it daily provision on our way to eternal life; through Jesus Christ our Lord. AMEN.

IV

O SON of God eternal, who, taking man's flesh upon Thee, didst endure for us the outrage of the Cross; by the mystery of Thy passion free us from eternal death, and, as by Thy dying and rising again Thou hast rescued us from darkness, so, when Thou comest to judgment in Thy kingdom, deliver us from blame; who livest and reignest with the Father and the Holy Ghost, God blessed for ever. AMEN.

PALM SUNDAY

WHEN the time was come for the Lord Jesus to be received up, He steadfastly set His face to go to Jerusalem. Today we remember His triumphal entry as King into the Holy City, as the prophets had foretold.

BLESSED is He that cometh in the name of the Lord. Hosanna in the highest.

Behold the Lamb of God which taketh away the sin of the world.

I

ASSIST us mercifully with Thy help, O Lord God of our salvation; that we may approach with reverence to the meditation of those mighty acts whereby Thou hast given us life and immortality; through Jesus Christ our Lord. AMEN.

Let us confess our sins unto Almighty God.

ALMIGHTY God, we bow down before Thee, acknowledging our unworthiness and our sin. Thou didst send Thy Son to shew us the way of life, yet we have erred from it continually. Thou hast manifested His kingly right, and we have seen His glory; yet, while offering Him the homage of our lips, we have not given Him the loyalty of our lives. We have followed our own pleasures; we have sought our own ends; we have lived in selfishness; we have refused the way of the Cross. Have mercy upon us; rebuke our waywardness and folly, and grant us true repentance, that our sins may be forgiven.

Almighty and everlasting God, who hatest nothing that Thou hast made, and dost forgive the sins of all them that are penitent; create and make in us new and contrite hearts, that we worthily lamenting our sins, and acknowledging our wretchedness, may obtain of Thee, the God of all mercy, perfect remission and forgiveness; through Jesus Christ our Lord. AMEN.

Let us pray, as we remember His Passion, that God may deepen our lives in Christ.

HELP us, we humbly beseech Thee, in these holy days to enter into the secret place of the Most High. Let the noise of the world be hushed, that we may hear Thy voice. Teach us to wait upon Thee. Teach us to glory in the Cross of Jesus Christ, and to lay down our life that we may find it again; and bring us into the fellowship of that love which endured the Cross, despising the shame; through the same Jesus Christ our Lord. AMEN.

O LORD Jesus Christ, who as on this day didst enter the rebellious city where Thou wast to die; enter into our hearts, we beseech Thee, and subdue them wholly to Thyself. And, as Thy faithful disciples blessed Thy coming, and spread their garments in the way, covering it with palm branches; make us ready to lay at Thy feet all that we have and are, and to bless Thee, who comest in the name of the Lord. And grant that after we have confessed and worshipped Thee on earth, we may be among the number of those who at the last shall hail Thine eternal triumph, and bear in their hands the palms of victory, when every knee shall

bow before Thee, and every tongue confess that
Thou art Lord, to the glory of God the Father.
AMEN.

ALMIGHTY and everlasting God, who, of Thy
tender love towards mankind, hast sent Thy
Son, our Saviour Jesus Christ, to take upon Him
our flesh, and to suffer death upon the Cross, that
all mankind should follow the example of His great
humility; mercifully grant, that we may both follow
the example of His patience, and also be made partakers of His resurrection; through the same Jesus
Christ our Lord. AMEN.

II

Let us lift up our hearts, and give thanks unto
our Lord God.

IT is verily meet, right, and our bounden duty
that we should at all times and in all places give
thanks unto Thee, O Holy Lord, Father Almighty,
Everlasting God. We magnify Thy name for Thine
unspeakable gift in Jesus Christ Thy Son, and for
Thy purpose of love towards men which He came
to fulfil. More especially this day we praise Thee
for the faithfulness with which He trod the way of
suffering, and the grace with which He endured
the contradiction of sinners. For His gentleness
under provocation, His patience under affliction,
His meekness alike in honour and in contempt, we
bless Thee; for the Cross which He carried, and the
death which He died, we praise Thee without end.
Therefore with angels and archangels, and with all
the company of heaven, we laud and magnify Thy
glorious name; evermore praising Thee and saying:

HOLY, Holy, Holy, Lord God of Hosts,
Heaven and earth are full of Thy glory:
Glory be to Thee, O Lord most high.

BLESSED is He that cometh in the name of the
Lord: Hosanna in the highest.

O GOD, we beseech Thee that all who behold
Thy Son in His passion may surrender themselves to Him and follow in His steps. Give Thy
Church courage to declare His right to reign, and to
proclaim Him Lord of all. Strengthen and uphold
Thy servants who set forth the word of the Cross;
and when they suffer scorn and rejection, give them
grace to endure as seeing Him who is invisible.

We pray for our Queen and country. Cast out from
among us whatsoever is displeasing in Thy sight,
and help us to order all our affairs to Thy glory.

Look in mercy upon the nations of men, and
grant that all tyrannies may be dethroned, all evils
destroyed, and righteousness and peace prevail
throughout the world.

Almighty and everlasting God, who drivest none
from Thy mercy, we pray for the Jews, that Thou
wouldest remove the veil from their hearts, that so
they too may acknowledge our Lord Jesus Christ.

In the name of Him who accepted the Hosannas
of the children, we beseech Thee to bless all
children, and to direct those who teach them, that
they may ever honour Thy name.

We remember before Thee all who are in distress,
and those who are nigh unto death. Set Thou Thy
Cross, O Christ, between their souls and their sins.
Illumine for them the road to death, and bring
them at last into Thine everlasting habitations.

We commend to Thy keeping all our loved ones

especially those who are far away from us, whom we name in silence before Thee, . . . that they and we may be united in the memory of that love which sought us even through the agony of death; through Jesus Christ our Lord. AMEN.

ALMIGHTY God, who art the God not of the dead but of the living; we praise Thy name for all who have lived and died in faith, and are now at rest with Thee; making especial remembrance before Thee of those ever dear to ourselves; . . . help us like them to follow Christ, that at the last we may receive with them the end of our faith, life full and everlasting; through Jesus Christ our Lord, who liveth and reigneth with Thee and the Holy Spirit, one eternal God, world without end. AMEN.

III

O LORD Jesus Christ, Son of the Living God, who for our redemption didst die upon the Cross the most shameful of deaths; grant us now Thy holy Spirit as we remember Thy sufferings; and by Thy holy Cross bring us at the last to that realm of eternal joy, where Thou livest and reignest with the Father and the same Spirit, ever one God, world without end. AMEN.

IV

O LORD, make us perfect in Christ Jesus; out of His fullness may we all receive, and rest in Him for evermore. May His passion be our deliverance, His wounds our healing, His Cross our redemption, and His death our life. Suffering with Him here may we reign with Him hereafter, and bearing now His Cross may we hereafter wear His crown; through the same Jesus Christ our Lord. AMEN.

HOLY WEEK

MONDAY IN HOLY WEEK

ON this day our Lord returned from Bethany to Jerusalem, cursing the barren fig-tree on the way. He cleansed the courts of the Temple, and declared that His Father's House should be a house of prayer for all nations.

IN the name of the Father and of the Son and of the Holy Ghost. AMEN.

Let us pray.

ALMIGHTY God, we beseech Thee graciously to behold this Thy family, for which our Lord Jesus Christ was contented to be betrayed, and given up into the hands of wicked men, and to suffer death upon the Cross, who now liveth and reigneth with Thee and the Holy Ghost, ever one God, world without end. AMEN.

ALMIGHTY and everlasting God, who hatest nothing that Thou hast made, and dost forgive the sins of all them that are penitent; create and make in us new and contrite hearts, that we

Note. These services are designed to be brief and of an intensely devotional character. Where there is an adequate choir another singing may be introduced, and where it is preferred the services may commence with praise. The Prose Psalms may be chanted or said. Where they are said, it is recommended that the Minister read the first part of each verse (generally terminated by a double bar in the pointed edition of the Psalter) and the Congregation the second.

worthily lamenting our sins, and acknowledging our wretchedness, may obtain of Thee, the God of all mercy, perfect remission and forgiveness; through Jesus Christ our Lord. AMEN.

ASSIST us mercifully with Thy help, O Lord God of our salvation, that we may approach with reverence to the meditation of those mighty acts whereby Thou hast given us life and immortality; through Jesus Christ our Lord. AMEN.

O SAVIOUR of the world who by Thy Cross and precious blood hast redeemed us, save us and help us, we humbly beseech Thee, O Lord. AMEN.

Prose Psalm xxvi or xxvii, read responsively.

O.T. Lesson: Jeremiah vii. 1–15.

N.T. Lesson: The record of this day, as it is delivered in the Gospel according to St. Mark xi. 12–26.

Para. xxx: Come let us to the Lord our God. *Tune* St. Fulbert.

The Apostles' Creed.

Let us pray.

O Lord hear our prayer:
And let our cry come unto Thee.

ALMIGHTY and everlasting God, who of Thy tender love towards mankind, hast sent Thy Son our Saviour Jesus Christ, to take upon Him our flesh, and to suffer death upon the Cross, that all mankind should follow the example of His great humility; mercifully grant that we may both follow the example of His patience, and also be made partakers of His resurrection; through the same Jesus Christ our Lord. AMEN.

ALMIGHTY God, whose blessed Son Jesus
Christ did as on this day curse the barren fig-
tree, deliver us, we beseech Thee, from all unfruit-
fulness in His service, and give us grace to bring
forth abundantly the fruits of righteousness, love,
and true obedience; and as on this day He did
cleanse the courts of Thy holy house, so do Thou
purify our hearts from all defilement, our worship
from all insincerity, and our lives from all hypo-
crisy, that we may be the Temple of the living God,
and that Thy Holy Spirit may dwell within us;
through the same Jesus Christ our Lord. AMEN.

Hymn: Lord as to Thy dear Cross we flee.

Address.

Hymn: O Lord and Master of us all.

Let us pray.

LORD have mercy upon us.
Christ have mercy upon us.
Lord have mercy upon us.

*Here may follow, if it be thought desirable, these
intercessions.*

O GOD, whose will it is that Thy Church be
holy; cause Thy people to remember that
wheresoever Christ may come, judgment begins at
Thine own house; that we may cleanse our hearts
of everything that defileth, and sanctify our worship and our works before Thee.

O merciful God who lovest all; have mercy on
Thine ancient people Israel, and upon all who deny
the faith of Christ crucified. Take from them all
ignorance and contempt of Thy word, so that they
with us may be one flock under one Shepherd.

Remember all whom we love, and keep them steadfast in Thy faith. Support the old by Thy strength; keep the young by Thy loving watchfulness; comfort the sick and sorrowful; give Thy peace to the dying; preserve us and all Thy saints in one communion and fellowship, that we may ever praise and glorify Thee, Father, Son, and Holy Spirit, one God, blessed for ever. AMEN.

OUR Father . . .

THE grace of our Lord Jesus Christ, and the love of God and the fellowship of the Holy Ghost, be with us all. AMEN.

TUESDAY IN HOLY WEEK

ON Tuesday our Lord spake the Parables of the Two Sons, the Wicked Husbandmen, the Marriage Supper, the Ten Virgins, and the Talents. He answered the questionings of the Pharisees, Sadducees, and a certain lawyer. He foretold the destruction of Jerusalem, and described the Last Judgment of men.

IN the name of the Father and of the Son and of the Holy Ghost. AMEN.

Let us pray.

O LORD Jesus, our most adorable Saviour, behold us at Thy feet, imploring Thy mercy for ourselves and for all men. Vouchsafe to apply to us the merits of Thy passion to which our meditation is directed; and grant that while we trace Thy way of conflict and sorrow our hearts may be touched with true contrition for our sins, and learn to accept with cheerfulness whatsoever Thou requirest of us whether to do or to endure. AMEN.

ALMIGHTY and everlasting God, who hatest nothing that Thou hast made, and dost forgive the sins of all them that are penitent; create and make in us new and contrite hearts, that we worthily lamenting our sins, and acknowledging our wretchedness, may obtain of Thee, the God of all mercy, perfect remission and forgiveness; through Jesus Christ our Lord. AMEN.

ASSIST us mercifully with Thy help, O Lord God of our salvation, that we may approach with reverence to the meditation of those mighty acts whereby Thou hast given us life and immortality; through Jesus Christ our Lord. AMEN.

O SAVIOUR of the world, who by Thy Cross and precious blood hast redeemed us, save us and help us, we humbly beseech Thee, O Lord. AMEN.

Prose Psalm lvi, read responsively.

The record of the day as it is delivered in the Gospel according to St. Mark xi. 20–2, xii.

Psalm cxxx: Lord from the depths. *Tune* Martyrdom.

The Apostles' Creed.

Let us pray.

O LORD hear our prayer:
And let our cry come unto Thee.

ALMIGHTY and everlasting God, who of Thy tender love towards mankind hast sent Thy Son our Saviour Jesus Christ, to take upon Him our flesh, and to suffer death upon the Cross, that all mankind should follow the example of His great humility; mercifully grant that we may both follow the example of His patience, and also be made partakers of His resurrection; through the same Jesus Christ our Lord. AMEN.

ALMIGHTY God, whose blessed Son Jesus Christ did as on this day utter the great parables of watchfulness and faithfulness and judgment to come, grant us grace, we beseech Thee, to be ever watchful for His coming and diligent in His work; and as on this day He did enter into controversy with sinful men and endure the contradiction of sinners against Himself, grant that we may never try His patience nor provoke His wrath, but may learn of Him, the meek and lowly of heart, to be gentle and patient and true, that, when He cometh to judge the world, we may receive the blessing from His lips: Come, ye blessed of My Father, inherit the kingdom prepared for you; through the same Jesus Christ our Lord. AMEN.

Hymn: There is a green hill.

Address.

Hymn: There is a fountain filled with blood.

Let us pray.

LORD have mercy upon us.
    Christ have mercy upon us.
Lord have mercy upon us.

Here may follow, if it be thought desirable, these intercessions.

O GOD, who willest that all men should know and see Thee in Thy Son; we pray for Thy holy Church throughout the world, that Thou wouldst keep her pure from all superstition and error, and grant to her a right understanding of Thy will, and faithfulness in witnessing to the truth as it is in Jesus.

We pray for those who are weak and unstable in faith, and for those who are entangled in strife and debate by them that believe not. Grant them the spirit of power, love, and a sound mind, that they may fearlessly declare the truth, and bear the reproach of Christ their Master.

O Lord Jesus Christ, who camest to bear the sicknesses and carry the sorrows of men; manifest Thy healing power, we beseech Thee, to the sick in body or mind. Speak peace to the troubled; strengthen the weak; succour and relieve those who have no helper; and lead all in tribulation by the waters of comfort and the ways of righteousness to Thy kingdom of rest and glory.

O God, from whom all holy desires, all good counsels, and all just works do proceed; give unto Thy servants that peace which the world cannot give; that both our hearts may be set to obey Thy commandments, and also that by Thee we being defended from the fear of our enemies may pass our time in rest and quietness; through the merits of Jesus Christ our Saviour. AMEN.

OUR Father . . .

THE grace of our Lord Jesus Christ, and the love of God, and the fellowship of the Holy Ghost, be with us all. AMEN.

WEDNESDAY IN HOLY WEEK

ON this day our Lord remained withdrawn in silence in Bethany preparing Himself for the agony that awaited Him, while Judas was bargaining with the chief priests to betray Him.

IN the name of the Father and of the Son and of the Holy Ghost. AMEN.

Let us pray.

ALMIGHTY God, we beseech Thee graciously to behold this Thy family, for which our Lord Jesus Christ was contented to be betrayed, and given up into the hands of wicked men, and to suffer death upon the Cross, who now liveth and reigneth with Thee and the Holy Ghost, ever one God, world without end. AMEN.

ALMIGHTY and everlasting God, who hatest nothing that Thou hast made, and dost forgive the sins of all them that are penitent; create and make in us new and contrite hearts, that we worthily lamenting our sins, and acknowledging our wretchedness, may obtain of Thee, the God of all mercy, perfect remission and forgiveness; through Jesus Christ our Lord. AMEN.

ALMIGHTY and everlasting God, the Creator of the ends of the earth, who givest power to the faint and renewest strength unto them that wait upon Thee; look in compassion unto us who trust in Thy mercy. As we remember how our Saviour sought strength in Thy presence for the trial of His faith, we pray Thee to give us like faith to wait upon Thee, that we may find courage and strength to do and to endure what Thou hast appointed for us; through the same Jesus Christ our Lord. AMEN.

O SAVIOUR of the world who by Thy Cross and precious blood hast redeemed us, save us and help us, we humbly beseech Thee, O Lord. AMEN.

Prose Psalm xl, read responsively.

Lesson: The record of the day as it is delivered in the Gospel according to St. Mark xiv. 1–11.

Psalm cxvi. 1–7. I love the Lord. *Tune* Kilmarnock.

The Apostles' Creed.

Let us pray.

O LORD hear our prayer:
  And let our cry come unto Thee.

A LMIGHTY and everlasting God, who of Thy tender love towards mankind, hast sent Thy Son our Saviour Jesus Christ, to take upon Him our flesh, and to suffer death upon the Cross, that all mankind should follow the example of His great humility; mercifully grant that we may both follow the example of His patience, and also be made partakers of His resurrection; through the same Jesus Christ our Lord. AMEN.

A LMIGHTY God, whose blessed Son Jesus Christ did as on this day withdraw Himself into the silence and seclusion of Bethany and prepare Himself in quietness for the struggle that was

to come; give unto us, we beseech Thee, the same
spirit of submission and endurance that was in
Him, and draw us closer into the fellowship of His
suffering and the communion of Thy sacred presence, that we may be strengthened thereby for all
the trials and temptations that lie before us, and
by His power may be more than conquerors;
through the same Jesus Christ our Lord. AMEN.

ALMIGHTY God, who to redeem lost mankind
didst suffer Thine only-begotten Son as on
this day to be betrayed by one of His own disciples into the hands of His enemies; mercifully
grant that we may never fall from Thee through
covetousness or any other temptation, but that we
may steadfastly persevere to the end, and finally
receive the crown of life; through the same Jesus
Christ our Lord. AMEN.

Hymn: Art thou weary.

Address.

Hymn: Peace, perfect peace.

Let us pray.

LORD have mercy upon us.
Christ have mercy upon us.
Lord have mercy upon us.

*Here may follow, if it be thought desirable, these inter-
cessions.*

LOOK, O Lord, in mercy upon Thy holy Church,
and confirm and strengthen her ministers.
Unite us all in the bonds of faith and love, and
guide us in the way of righteousness. Support the

aged, teach the young, convert the unbeliever, and forgive the penitent. Give health to the sick, comfort to the sorrowful, liberty to the captives.

Hear us as we pray for those who have been overcome by temptation, who have drifted from the faith and cast away their confidence in Thee. Bring to their remembrance the passion of Christ, that they may cast themselves anew on Thy mercy, and never more depart from Thee.

Lighten our darkness, we beseech Thee, O Lord; and by Thy great mercy defend us from all perils and dangers of this night; for the love of Thy only Son, our Saviour, Jesus Christ. AMEN.

OUR Father . . .

THE grace of our Lord Jesus Christ, and the love of God, and the fellowship of the Holy Ghost, be with us all. AMEN.

THURSDAY IN HOLY WEEK

ON this day our Lord went again to Jerusalem. In the evening in the Upper Room, He washed the feet of the disciples, and instituted the blessed Sacrament of His Body and Blood. He spoke the words of comfort and peace, gave the promise of the coming of the Holy Spirit, and made the great intercession. In the Garden of Gethsemane He endured His agony. Betrayed by Judas and arrested by His enemies, He was taken to prison and to judgment.

IN the name of the Father and of the Son and of the Holy Ghost. AMEN.

Let us pray.

ETERNAL and ever-blessed God, who in Thine infinite compassion for weak and erring men didst not spare Thine own Son, but didst deliver Him up for us all; give us reverence, humility, and faith, as we approach the mystery of His agony, that we may enter into the fellowship of His sufferings, and that our sins may be forgiven; for His name's sake, even Jesus Christ our Lord. AMEN.

ASSIST us mercifully with Thy help, O Lord God of our salvation, that we may approach with reverence to the meditation of those mighty acts whereby Thou hast given us life and immortality; through Jesus Christ our Lord. AMEN.

O SAVIOUR of the world who by Thy Cross and precious blood hast redeemed us, save us and help us, we humbly beseech Thee, O Lord. AMEN.

Prose Psalm cxliii, read responsively.

Lesson: The record of the Upper Room, as it is delivered in the Gospel according to St. John xiii. 1–17, and in the Gospel according to St. Luke xxii. 15–22.

Para. xxxv: 'Twas on that night. *Tune* Rockingham.

Lesson: The record of the Garden of Gethsemane, as it is delivered in the Gospel according to St. Matthew xxvi. 36–56.

The Apostles' Creed.

Let us pray.

O LORD hear our prayer:
    And let our cry come unto Thee.

E

O LORD Jesus Christ, enthroned in the majesty of heaven, who, when Thou camest forth from God, didst make Thyself as one that serveth; we adore Thee because Thou didst lay aside the garment of Thy glory, and gird Thyself with lowliest humility and minister to Thy disciples, washing their feet. Teach us to know what Thou hast done and to follow Thine example; deliver us from pride, jealousy, and ambition, and make us ready to be subject one to another, and with lowliness to serve one another for Thy sake, O Jesus Christ, our Lord and Saviour. AMEN.

ALMIGHTY God, whose blessed Son Jesus Christ did as on this day ordain in the holy Sacrament the perpetual Memorial of His death and the Communion of His risen life; grant that when in obedience to Thy command, we keep the feast, we may approach Thy table with love and humble hope; that, discerning its sacred mystery, we may feed by faith on His body and blood, and be made partakers of Thy heavenly grace; through the same Jesus Christ our Lord. AMEN.

ALMIGHTY God, whose blessed Son Jesus Christ did as on this day endure the dread agony of Gethsemane, when His soul was exceeding sorrowful even unto death; give us grace to know that our sins were the cause of His sorrow, and that our guilt weighed Him down and filled His soul with anguish; and grant us, we beseech Thee, to have such abhorrence of all evil, that we may suffer with Him in His sorrow; teach us to watch and pray that we may be kept through the hour of temptation; and give us such willingness of spirit, strength of heart, and patient quietness, that we may not shrink from drinking His cup, nor fail Him in His hour of trial; through the same Jesus Christ our Lord. AMEN.

Hymn: Christian, seek not yet repose.

Address.

Hymn: In the hour of trial.

Let us pray.

LORD have mercy upon us.
Christ have mercy upon us
Lord have mercy upon us.

Here may follow, if it be thought desirable, these intercessions.

ALMIGHTY God, who art calling Thy whole family to remembrance of Him who loved the Church and gave Himself for it; we beseech Thee that all who name the name of Christ may be moved to penitence for their divisions, and be drawn to seek that unity and peace for which as on this night He prayed.

Lift up the eyes of men in all nations, that they may behold in Him their salvation and their peace.

We pray for all who find life hard and faith difficult, that, trusting in Thee, they may be of a good courage.

We pray for those who are falsely accused, that they may, even as their Lord, endure reproach with meekness, and, committing their way unto Him, be assured that He will bring forth their righteousness as the light.

We pray for those who suffer persecution for Christ's sake, that, in nothing terrified by their enemies, they may be bold on behalf of their Lord.

We pray for those who are tempted to deny their Master, that Thou wilt strengthen them that they may stand, and enable them to hold fast to Him who was tempted, yet overcame.

We pray for those who have departed from Thee, that by the power of Thy love Thou wilt draw them back, restore their faith, and establish their way; through Jesus Christ our Lord. AMEN.

CHRIST became obedient unto death . . .

Have mercy upon me, O God, according to Thy loving-kindness; according unto the multitude of Thy tender mercies, blot out my transgressions. Wash me throughly from mine iniquity; and cleanse me from my sin. Create in me a clean heart, O God, and renew a right spirit within me. The sacrifices of God are a broken spirit; a broken and a contrite heart, O God, Thou wilt not despise.

Christ became obedient unto death . . .

O God, whose blessed Son did suffer for all mankind; grant unto us that, rightly observing this holy season, we may learn to know Thee better, to love Thee more, and to serve Thee with a more perfect will; through the same Jesus Christ our Lord. AMEN.

OUR Father . . .

THE grace of our Lord Jesus Christ, the love of God, and the fellowship of the Holy Ghost, be with us all. AMEN.

GOOD FRIDAY
Morning

ON this day our Lord was tried before the High Priests, then by Pilate, thereafter by Herod, and then by Pilate again; was scourged, mocked, and condemned to death. He was led out to Calvary. At nine o'clock He was crucified. At intervals He spoke the first three words from the Cross. From twelve o'clock till three He endured the darkness of dereliction. At three o'clock, having uttered the other four words from the Cross, He bowed His head and died.

Is it nothing to you, all ye that pass by? Behold and see if there be any sorrow like unto My sorrow, wherewith the Lord hath afflicted Me.

I, if I be lifted up from the earth, will draw all men unto Me.

Let us pray.

O LORD Jesus Christ, there was never sorrow like unto Thy sorrow: Thy soul was exceeding sorrowful, even unto death. The cruel soldiers scourged Thee; they smote, they spat upon Thy sacred face. Over Thee in derision they threw the purple robe, and forced the crown of thorns upon Thy head, Thou King and Lord of all. They led Thee forth to the place of death, bearing Thy Cross. They pierced Thy hands and Thy feet; they nailed Thee to the Tree. Thou wast lifted up between heaven and earth as utterly unworthy, despised and rejected of men. None gave Thee love or pity, who wast full of love and pity for all.

O Lord, we behold Thy sufferings, and we mourn: we weep not for Thee, but for ourselves; for Thou wast wounded for our transgressions,

Thou wast bruised for our iniquities. And above all we mourn that, although we have been made partakers of Thy grace, our sins have pierced Thee anew; we have seemed to count Thy sacrifice a vain thing; we have forgotten that we were cleansed from our old sins. They who nailed Thee to the Cross knew not that they crucified the King of Glory; but we have known, and yet we have crucified Thee afresh, and put Thee to an open shame.

Yet, Lord Jesus, let not Thy mercy fail; and as in Thine hour of agony Thou didst pray for them that put Thee to death, so for us also do Thou intercede. O Saviour of the world, who by Thy Cross and precious blood hast redeemed us, save us and help us, we humbly beseech Thee, O Lord.

Behold, we wait before Thy Cross. We adore Thee, O Thou who wast crucified. Draw us to Thyself; conform us to Thine example; give unto us the spirit of meekness and patience in which Thou didst endure; and now and henceforth enable us to take up our Cross and follow Thee even unto the end.

And unto Thee, O blessed Saviour, with the Father and the Holy Ghost, we ascribe all glory for ever and ever. AMEN.

Hymn: O come and mourn with me awhile.

Lesson: The passion of our Lord and Saviour Jesus Christ as it is recorded in the Gospel according to St. John xviii. 1–27.

Hymn: O Saviour where shall guilty man.

Lesson: The continuation of the record of the passion of our Lord and Saviour Jesus Christ in the Gospel according to St. John xviii. 28–40.

Psalm xxiii: The Lord's my shepherd. *Tune* Wiltshire.

Lesson: The continuation, &c.—St. John xix. 1–24.

Hymn: Throned upon the awful tree.

Lesson: The continuation, &c.—St. John xix. 25–37.

Hymn: There is a green hill.

The Apostles' Creed.

ALMIGHTY God, we beseech Thee graciously to behold this Thy family, for which our Lord Jesus Christ was contented to be betrayed, and given up into the hands of wicked men, and to suffer death upon the Cross, who now liveth and reigneth with Thee and the Holy Ghost, ever one God, world without end. AMEN.

O THOU, who hast purchased Thy Church unto Thyself with the precious blood of Thine own Son, hear us, we beseech Thee, for the whole congregation of the faithful; that all who believe in Thee in every place may be kept in unity of faith and in purity of love; that they may be preserved in peace from all the assaults of the devil, the world, and the flesh; and that persevering steadfastly therein they may be presented without spot or wrinkle, holy and unblamable, in the day of Jesus Christ; through the same Jesus Christ our Lord. AMEN.

O GOD of Abraham, of Isaac, and of Jacob, have mercy, we beseech Thee, upon Thine ancient people, the house of Israel. Deliver them from their hardness of heart and unbelief of Thy Gospel; that, their hearts being turned unto Thee, they may behold Thy glory in the face of Jesus Christ, and may acknowledge Him to be their Saviour, whom as on this day their fathers gave up to be crucified; that so they may be brought into Thy holy Church, and saved among the remnant of the true Israel; through the same Jesus Christ our Lord. AMEN.

O GOD and Father of all the families of the earth, who wouldst not that any should perish, but that all should come to the knowledge of the truth; we beseech Thee to have mercy upon those who are walking in darkness and bowing down to idols. Deliver them, we pray Thee, from all the delusions of the devil; bring them to know Thee, the only true God, and Jesus Christ whom Thou hast sent; and unite them to Thy true spiritual fold; through the same Jesus Christ our Lord. AMEN.

O MERCIFUL Father, the Comfort of those who are in sorrow, the Strength of those who are oppressed, let the cries of the afflicted enter into Thine ears we beseech Thee, and do Thou save them out of all their distresses. Heal Thou all who are sick; relieve all who are in need; and in Thy pity grant Thy consolations to all who are oppressed with grief; through Jesus Christ our Lord. AMEN.

Here a short address may be given.

Hymn: Sing my tongue how glorious battle *or* When I survey the wondrous Cross.

Let us pray.

CHRIST became obedient unto death . . .

HAVE mercy upon me, O God, according to Thy loving-kindness; according unto the multitude of Thy tender mercies blot out my transgressions.

Wash me throughly from mine iniquity; and cleanse me from my sin. Create in me a clean heart, O God, and renew a right spirit within me. The sacrifices of God are a broken spirit; a broken and a contrite heart Thou wilt not despise. AMEN.

Christ became obedient unto death . . .

OUR Father . . .

THE grace of our Lord Jesus Christ, and the love of God, and the fellowship of the Holy Ghost, be with us all. AMEN.

GOOD FRIDAY

A Devotion on the Seven Words

O LORD Jesus Christ, Son of the Father and Saviour of the world, hear us as with humble and adoring hearts we remember Thy seven words of love spoken on this day from the Cross. Draw us, we beseech Thee, into closer communion with Thy Spirit, that the mind which was in Thee may also be found in us.

We remember that, as they crucified Thee, Thou didst say, FATHER FORGIVE THEM, FOR THEY KNOW NOT WHAT THEY DO.

If Thou, Lord, shouldst mark iniquities, O Lord who shall stand? But there is forgiveness with Thee that Thou mayest be feared. Thou thine own self didst bear our sins in Thine own body on the Tree that we, being dead to sin, should live unto righteousness.

Wherefore we worship and adore Thy holy name. AMEN.

WE remember Thy promise unto the penitent thief, VERILY, I SAY UNTO THEE, TODAY SHALT THOU BE WITH ME IN PARADISE.

With Thee, O Lord, is the fountain of life, and in Thy light shall we see light. O Shepherd of the flock of God, who guidest those who know Thy voice in green pastures and beside the waters of comfort, when we awake we shall be satisfied with Thy likeness.

Wherefore we worship and adore Thy holy name. AMEN.

WE remember Thy word unto Thy Mother and the disciple of Thy love, WOMAN, BEHOLD THY SON! BEHOLD THY MOTHER!

O Son of Man who camest to revive the spirit of the humble, and to bind up the broken in heart; Thy loving-kindness is better than life, therefore my lips shall praise Thee. My soul doth magnify Thee, O Lord, and my spirit doth rejoice in God my Saviour.

Wherefore we worship and adore Thy holy name. AMEN.

WE remember the loneliness of that loud cry which burst from Thine over-burdened heart, while the dread darkness lay upon the land, MY GOD, MY GOD, WHY HAST THOU FORSAKEN ME?

O Son of God, beloved of the Father, was ever sorrow like unto Thy sorrow? Thou wast despised and rejected of men, a man of sorrows and acquainted with grief. For our transgressions Thou wast wounded; for our iniquities Thou wast bruised; the chastisement of our peace was upon Thee, and with Thy stripes we are healed. All we, like sheep, had gone astray. We had turned every one to his own way, and God the Father laid on Thee the iniquity of us all.

Wherefore we worship and adore Thy holy name. AMEN.

WE remember how, in fulfilment of the Scriptures, Thou didst say I THIRST.

Was it not written of Thee, My strength is dried up like a potsherd, and my tongue cleaveth to my jaws, and Thou hast brought me into the dust of death? Yet Thy word endureth. If any man thirst, let him come unto Me and drink. O Thou fount of life, who thirsteth for the souls of men, my soul thirsteth for Thee in a dry and thirsty land, where no water is.

Wherefore we worship and adore Thy holy name. AMEN.

WE remember that word which from Thy lips alone was very truth, IT IS FINISHED.

O Alpha and Omega, the Beginning and the End, the Author and Finisher of the Faith, for the joy that was set before Thee Thou didst endure the Cross, despising the shame, and art now set down at the right hand of the throne on high.

Wherefore we worship and adore Thy holy name. AMEN.

WE remember that, when Thou hadst cried with a loud voice, Thou didst say, FATHER, INTO THY HANDS I COMMEND MY SPIRIT, and then, bowing Thy head, Thou gavest up the ghost.

O Saviour of the world, whom have I in heaven but Thee? And there is none upon earth that I desire beside Thee. My flesh and my heart faileth;

but God is the strength of my heart, and my portion for ever. Into Thy hands I commit my spirit; Thou hast redeemed me, O Lord God of truth.

Wherefore we worship and adore Thy holy name, saying Worthy art Thou, O Lamb that wast slain, to receive power, and riches and wisdom and strength, and honour, and glory and blessing.

Blessing and honour, and glory, and power, be unto Him that sitteth upon the throne, and unto the Lamb, for ever and ever. AMEN.

GOOD FRIDAY

Evening

CHRIST became obedient unto death, even the death of the Cross.

God forbid that I should glory save in the cross of our Lord Jesus Christ.

IN the name of the Father and of the Son and of the Holy Ghost. AMEN.

Let us pray.

ALMIGHTY God, we beseech Thee graciously to behold this Thy family, for which our Lord Jesus Christ was contented to be betrayed, and given up into the hands of wicked men, and to suffer death upon the Cross, who now liveth and reigneth with Thee and the Holy Ghost, ever one God, world without end. AMEN.

O SAVIOUR of the world, who by Thy Cross and precious blood hast redeemed us, save us and help us, we humbly beseech Thee O Lord. AMEN.

Psalm cxliii (2), *6–8:* Lo! I do stretch my hands.
Tune Leuchars.

Let us pray.

WE confess unto Thee, O God Almighty, Father, Son and Holy Ghost, and before all the company of heaven, that we have sinned, in thought, in word, and in deed, through our fault, through our own fault, through our own most grievous fault. Wherefore we pray Thee, O God, to have mercy upon us.

Almighty God, most merciful Father, grant us pardon, absolution and remission of all our sins; through the merit and mediation of Jesus Christ our Lord. AMEN.

LOOK down, O Lord, from Thy heavenly throne, illuminate the darkness of this night with Thy celestial brightness, and from the sons of light banish the deeds of darkness; through Jesus Christ our Lord. AMEN.

O LORD God, whose blessed Son did bear our sins in His own body on the Tree; give us, we pray Thee, such true repentance and amendment of life, that we may never crucify Him afresh, and put Him to an open shame by conscious and wilful sin; through the same Jesus Christ our Lord. AMEN.

OUR Father . . .

Hymn: O Sacred Head sore wounded.

Lesson: St. Matthew xxvii. 33–61.

Para. xliv: 'Tis finished—was His latest voice. *Tune* Gloucester.

Or,

Hymn: Praise to the Holiest.

Let us pray.

O BLESSED Lord Jesus Christ, who for the work of our salvation didst humble Thyself to die for us, and also to be buried; we magnify Thee, Thou Giver of life, and reverence Thy passion and Thy burial. When they had fulfilled all that was written of Thee, they took Thee down from the Cross, and laid Thee in a sepulchre. But Thy flesh did rest in hope, for God left not Thy soul in hell, neither did He suffer His holy One to see corruption.

O Thou holy and spotless Lamb, we unite with all the heavenly host in ascribing unto Thee power, and riches, and wisdom, and strength, and honour, and glory, and blessing. We bless Thee for all the burdens Thou hast borne, for all the tears Thou hast wept, for all the pains Thou hast suffered, for every word of comfort Thou hast spoken on the Cross, for every conflict with the powers of darkness, and for Thine eternal victory over the terrors of death and the pains of hell.

And now though we walk through the valley of the shadow of death we will fear no evil, for Thou art with us. Thou wilt show us the path of life; in Thy presence is fullness of joy; at Thy right hand are pleasures for evermore. Wherefore we magnify Thee, O Word of Life, with the Father and the Holy Ghost, one God, both now and for evermore. AMEN.

O GOD, let Thy whole Church be subdued and sanctified by the pitifulness of Thy great mercy.

Most merciful Father, we beseech Thee for all who have been carried away by the vanity of error, and have forsaken the congregation of Thy Church, that they may be restored to the knowledge of Thy truth as it is in Jesus, and in the unity of the faith grow up in all things into Jesus Christ our Head.

O God, who of old didst choose Thine ancient people, the house of Israel, that the promised Saviour might appear among them; we pray that the veil may be taken from their hearts, that they may behold Thy glory in the face of Jesus Christ, and acknowledge Him to be the Saviour, whom as on this day their fathers gave up to be crucified.

O God, the Father of all mankind, who wouldest not that any should perish, but that all should come to the knowledge of Thy truth; have mercy, we beseech Thee, upon those who are walking in the darkness of ignorance and error, and bring them to know Thee, and Jesus Christ whom Thou hast sent. Bestow Thy blessing upon all missionaries of the Cross; that the Crucified One may see of the travail of His soul and be satisfied. Turn the hearts of the peoples from all hatred, fear, and oppression, and let Thy reconciling Spirit triumph among the nations and races of mankind.

Merciful God, the comfort of all who sorrow, the strength of the oppressed; let the cries of the afflicted come unto Thee, and save them out of all their distresses. Heal those who are sick, relieve all who are in need, grant consolation to all oppressed with grief, and fill them with Thy peace.

Receive, we beseech Thee, these our petitions, which we present unto Thee in the name of Jesus Christ, our crucified Saviour. Accept and answer us for His sake, who liveth and reigneth, and is worshipped and glorified, with Thee, O Father, and with the Holy Spirit, world without end. AMEN.

Hymn: O perfect life of love.

Address.

Hymn: Rock of Ages.

Let us pray.

O GOD, who by the Cross and passion of Thy Son Jesus Christ didst save and deliver mankind; grant that by steadfast faith in the merits of that holy sacrifice we may find help and salvation, and may triumph in the power of His victory; through the same Jesus Christ our Lord. AMEN.

SAVE us, O Lord, waking, and guard us sleeping, that awake we may watch with Christ, and asleep we may rest in peace.

THE Lord Almighty grant us a quiet night and a perfect end.

UNTO God's gracious care and keeping I commit you. The Lord bless you and keep you; the Lord make His face shine upon you and be gracious unto you. The Lord lift up His countenance upon you, and give you peace.

And the blessing of God Almighty, Father, Son and Holy Ghost, be with you now and always. AMEN.

SATURDAY IN HOLY WEEK

IN the name of the Father and of the Son and of the Holy Ghost. AMEN.

Let us pray.

UNTO Thee, O Lord, do we return. Thou hast smitten and Thou wilt bind us up. Thou hast torn and Thou wilt heal us. Bring our soul out of prison that we may praise Thy name. O Lord our God, our soul is cast down within us. All Thy waves and Thy billows are gone over us. Yet command, O Lord, Thy loving-kindness in the daytime, and in the night Thy song to be with us, for our prayer is unto Thee, the God of our life.

ALMIGHTY and everlasting God, who hatest nothing that Thou hast made, and dost forgive the sins of all them that are penitent; create and make in us new and contrite hearts, that we worthily lamenting our sins and acknowledging our wretchedness, may obtain of Thee, the God of all mercy, perfect remission and forgiveness; through Jesus Christ our Lord. AMEN.

Prose Psalm xvi, read responsively.

Lessons: 1. 1 Peter iii. 18–22.
　　　　2. St. Matthew xxvii. 59–66.

Para. xxv. 11–16: Midst sinners low in dust He lay.
Tune St. Mary.

The Apostles' Creed.

Let us pray.

O LORD hear our prayer:
And let our cry come unto Thee.

O CHRIST, Thou eternal Word, who wast pleased to rest on the seventh day from the work of creation; who as on this day, having finished the work the Father gave Thee to do, didst rest in Paradise; who also hast graciously invited all that labour and are heavy laden to come unto Thee; receive us, we beseech Thee, unworthy sinners, weary and heavy laden; give us rest in our labour, comfort in sorrow and a place with Thy people, where Thou wilt wipe away the tears from off all faces; for Thine own name's sake, O Jesus Christ our Lord. AMEN.

O BLESSED Lord Jesus Christ, who for the work of our salvation didst humble Thyself to die for us and also to be buried; we beseech Thee that Thou wilt never forsake Thy mystical body the Church; but wilt so continually vouchsafe Thy presence unto Thy people, and visit them with the consolations of the Holy Ghost in the midst of the darkness of this world, that they may be kept in patient waiting for the glory of the resurrection, when Thou shalt appear again without sin unto salvation.

Grant, O Lord, that as we are baptized into the death of Thy blessed Son our Saviour Jesus Christ, so by continually mortifying our corrupt affections we may be buried with Him; and that, through the grave the gate of death, we may pass to our joyful resurrection; for His merits, who died, and was buried, and rose again for us, Thy Son Jesus Christ our Lord, who liveth and reigneth with Thee and the Holy Spirit, one God for evermore. AMEN.

Hymn: When our heads are bowed with woe.

Address.

Hymn: By Jesus' grave on either hand.

Let us pray.

LORD have mercy upon us.
Christ have mercy upon us.
Lord have mercy upon us.

Here may follow, if it be thought desirable, these inter-cessions:

HEAR us, O God, as we pray for the Church, purchased by the blood of Christ. Purify her from all error, unbelief, and want of faith, that she may ever be the pillar and ground of the truth; and grant that she may so lift up the Cross of Jesus that all men may turn to Him and be saved.

Behold, O God, in compassion, those who are afflicted and heavy-laden, and in Thy mercy wipe away all tears from their eyes. Hear us as we pray for the dying: cleanse them by Thy mercy from all evil; give them a peaceful passage through the valley of the shadow; and receive them to Thy habitations of light and peace.

O Lord our God, who for our sakes didst suffer Thy Son to die, and also to be buried; look with compassion upon those who mourn for their beloved whom they see no more; visit them with Thy consolation, that they may be kept in humble hope and patient waiting for the glory of the resurrection.

O God, who from the tomb of our Lord Jesus Christ hast caused life and immortality to shine forth; we remember before Thee with thanksgiving all who have served Thee here in faith and love, especially those dear to our own hearts, who now behold Thee face to face. Grant us to be faithful as they were faithful, that over us death may have no dominion and that hereafter we, with them, may have our portion in the things Thou hast prepared for them that love Thee; through Jesus Christ our Lord. AMEN.

CHRIST became obedient unto death, even the death of the Cross. Wherefore God also hath highly exalted Him, and given Him a name which is above every name, that at the name of Jesus every knee should bow, of things in heaven, and things in earth, and things under the earth; and that every tongue should confess that Jesus Christ is Lord, to the glory of God the Father.

O death, where is thy sting? O grave, where is thy victory? Thanks be to God who giveth us the victory through our Lord Jesus Christ. I will both lay me down in peace, and sleep; for Thou Lord only makest me dwell in safety.

What shall I render unto the Lord for all His benefits towards Me? I will take the cup of salvation, and call upon the name of the Lord. I will pay my vows unto the Lord in the presence of all His people.

OUR Father . . .

THE grace of our Lord Jesus Christ, and the love of God, and the fellowship of the Holy Ghost be with us all. AMEN.

EASTER DAY

TODAY we remember the glorious resurrection from the dead of our Lord and Saviour Jesus Christ. Now hath Christ been raised from the dead, and become the first-fruits of them that are asleep. He is risen, as He said. Come, let us offer our sacrifice of thanksgiving to Almighty God and pay Him our vows.

CHRIST our Passover is sacrificed for us, therefore let us keep the feast.

Christ being raised from the dead dieth no more: death hath no more dominion over Him.

Thanks be to God who giveth us the victory through our Lord Jesus Christ.

I

PRAISE be to Thee, O Father Almighty, who didst raise up Thy Son from the dead and give Him glory, that our faith and hope might be in Thee. Praise be to Thee, O Lord Jesus Christ, who as on this day didst bring life and immortality to light. Praise be to Thee, O Holy Spirit of God, who dost quicken us together with Christ, and shed abroad his love in our hearts, that we may rejoice in the hope of His glory. All praise and thanks, dominion and power, be unto Thee, O holy and blessed Trinity, now and for evermore. AMEN.

BLESSED Lord Jesus, Thou conqueror over death and hell, behold us as we come to worship Thee. Give us faith that, not having seen, we may yet believe; hear us as now we cry to Thee, my Lord and my God; and make us partakers of the beauty and joy of this day when Thou didst burst asunder the barriers of the grave and rise triumphant, alive for evermore. AMEN.

O ALMIGHTY God, who broughtest again from the dead our Lord Jesus; we acknowledge that we are unworthy of Thy redeeming grace. We have not always believed Thy promises, nor trusted in our living Lord. Forgetting his presence and redeeming power, we have been overcome of evil. We have not listened to the glad tidings of His victory over death, and have refused to be comforted.

But now in penitence we come to Thee, beseeching Thy forgiveness. Mercifully grant us absolution from our sins, and restore unto us the joy of Thy salvation; through the same Jesus Christ, our Lord and Saviour. AMEN.

A LMIGHTY God, Father of our Lord Jesus Christ, quicken us, we beseech Thee, by Thy mighty power, from the death of sin unto the life of righteousness, and cause us to set our affections on things above, so that we may at the last have part in the resurrection of the just, and in the glory of Thy heavenly kingdom, whither Jesus the forerunner is for us entered, where also He liveth and reigneth with Thee and the Holy Ghost, God blessed for ever. AMEN.

At Holy Communion

O LORD Jesus Christ our God, Bread of Life Eternal, who hast fed us with the spiritual food of Thy divine benefits; look now, we humbly beseech Thee, upon our prayers and thanksgivings. Be known unto us, O Lover of mankind, in the breaking of bread, that all who partake thereof may receive health and blessing both in body and soul. And to Thee we ascribe all glory, who, with Thy Father everlasting and Thy life-giving Spirit, livest and reignest, God for ever and ever. AMEN.

II

O GIVE thanks unto the Lord, for He is good; for His mercy endureth for ever. Let the redeemed of the Lord say so, whom He hath brought out of darkness and the shadow of death.

O GOD Most High, all praise and thanks be unto Thee, for the multitude of Thy loving-kindnesses to us and to all men. It is meet and right that we should praise Thee at all times, but chiefly this day we give glory to Thy name because Thou hast brought immortality to light, through the victory of Jesus Christ. With Thy whole Church we bless Thee that He took upon Him the form of a servant, and humbled Himself, becoming obedient unto death, even the death of the Cross, that He might shew forth Thy redeeming love. We bless Thee that, by raising Him from the dead, Thou hast declared Him the Son of God with power. We thank Thee that He, being raised from the dead, dieth no more, and that death hath no more dominion over Him. We praise Thee, that, having overcome the sharpness of death, He opened the kingdom of heaven to all believers; and that because He lives, we shall live also. Thanks be to Thee, O God, Who givest us the victory, through our Lord Jesus Christ. AMEN.

ALMIGHTY God, whose blessed Son Christ Jesus sent forth His apostles to make Him known unto all nations; fill Thy Church throughout the world with His risen power. Pour out Thy Spirit on those who are called to minister in His name. As they break the bread of life to others, let their own souls be nourished and sustained. Vouchsafe to all Thy people, that, abiding in Christ, their Life, they may bear fruit abundantly to His glory.

O God, who hast promised Thy son the uttermost parts of the earth for His possession; take away the veil from the heart of Thy people Israel, that they may behold the Messiah promised to the fathers; and hasten the day when the fullness of the gentiles shall be gathered in and all men shall know Him as Saviour and worship Him as Lord.

Let Thy mercy rest, we beseech Thee, upon our land and nation; upon our Queen, and all in authority under her; that we may lead a quiet and peaceable life in all godliness and honesty. Rule the hearts of men in all classes of the people. Rebuke the power of unbelief and superstition, and preserve to us Thy pure word, in its liberty and glory, to the end of days.

Merciful Father, we commend to Thee all who are in any wise afflicted. Relieve those who suffer; restore health and strength to those who are sick. In Christ, who is the Resurrection and the Life, let the heavy-laden find strength to endure, and those who are in the valley of the shadow see the light of life eternal. Give to those in sorrow or loneliness the assurance that nothing can ever separate them from Thy love, which is in Christ Jesus our Lord.

We pray for all those dear to us, especially those

from whom we are parted, whom we name in our
hearts before Thee . . . that they may rejoice with
us this day, and that they and we may be sustained
by the assurance that at the last we shall meet
together in that City, where awaits us the inheritance incorruptible and undefiled, that fadeth not
away; through Jesus Christ our Lord. AMEN.

FATHER of Mercies and God of all Comfort;
we thank Thee that Jesus Christ is risen from
the dead, and become the first-fruits of them that are
fallen asleep in Him. For Thy saints, martyrs, and
confessors of every age and land, and for all pure
and beautiful souls who have walked with us here in
gentleness and love, and have made known to us
Thy light, we thank Thee. Surrounded with so
great a cloud of witnesses, grant us with Christ to
die to sin, that in Him we may live only to Thee,
and in the end inherit the Kingdom prepared for
all who love Him, that where He is, there we also
may be with Him.

And unto Thee, O Father, with the Son, and the
Holy Ghost, be praise and glory, now and evermore. AMEN.

III

BLESSED Lord, who, after Thy passion, didst
show Thyself alive unto Thine apostles by
many infallible proofs, and didst speak unto them
of the things pertaining to the Kingdom of God;
speak unto us also, we beseech Thee, that, waiting
upon Thee in faith and hope, we may know Thy
will, and serve Thee acceptably all the days of our
life; who livest and reignest with the Father and
the Holy Spirit, ever one God, world without end,
AMEN.

IV

ALMIGHTY God, who broughtest again from the dead our Lord Jesus, the glorious Prince of Salvation, with everlasting victory over hell and the grave; grant us power, we beseech Thee, to rise with Him to newness of life, that we may overcome the world with the victory of faith; through the same Jesus Christ our Lord. AMEN.

Benediction

NOW the God of Peace, who brought again from the dead our Lord Jesus, that great Shepherd of the sheep, through the blood of the everlasting covenant, make you perfect in every good work to do His will, working in you that which is well pleasing in His sight, through Jesus Christ; to whom be glory for ever and ever. AMEN.

A SERVICE OF SEVEN LESSONS
FOR EASTER EVENING

The service shall open with praise, after which, the Congregation still standing, the Minister shall say:

CHRIST is risen! Lift up your heads, O ye gates, and the King of Glory shall come in.

Beloved in Christ, at this glad festival of hope and immortality let us in heart and mind stand in the garden of Resurrection, and hear the angel saying unto us: He is not here; He is risen.

Therefore let us read and mark in Holy Scripture the record of that wondrous victory whereby death is conquered and life and immortality are brought to light. But first let us pray for the needs of the whole world and in especial for peace amongst the nations and brotherhood within the Church of the Risen Lord. And let us remember all who are in sorrow on this glad day, all who mourn their loved ones, all who know distress or separation or want; all who know not the victorious Saviour or who by sin have grieved His heart. Finally, let us remember in the light of the Resurrection morn, all who rejoice with us, but upon another shore, and in a greater light, that multitude which no man can number, who fell asleep in the faith of the Risen Christ, and with whom in Him we are one for evermore.

Let us pray.

O GOD, the Creator and Preserver of all mankind, we humbly beseech Thee for all sorts and conditions of men; that Thou wouldest be pleased to make Thy ways known unto them, Thy saving health unto all nations. More especially, we pray for the good estate of the Catholic Church; that it may be so guided and governed by Thy good Spirit, that all who profess and call themselves Christians may be led into the way of truth, and hold the faith in unity of spirit, in the bond of peace, and in righteousness of life. Finally, we commend to Thy fatherly goodness all those, who are in any ways afflicted or distressed, in mind, body, or estate; that it may please Thee to comfort and relieve them, according to their several necessities, giving them patience under their sufferings, and a happy issue out of all their afflictions. And this we beg for Jesus Christ His sake. AMEN.

ETERNAL God, in whose perfect kingdom no sword is drawn but the sword of righteousness, and no strength known but the strength of love; we pray Thee so mightily to shed abroad Thy spirit, that all peoples and ranks may be gathered under one banner of the Prince of Peace, as children of one God and Father of all; through Jesus Christ our Lord. AMEN.

O ETERNAL Lord God, who holdest all souls in life; we beseech Thee to shed forth upon Thy whole Church in Paradise and on earth the bright beams of Thy light and heavenly comfort; that we, following the good example of those who have loved and served Thee here and are now at rest, may with them at the last enter into the fullness of Thine unending joy; through Jesus Christ our Lord. AMEN.

THESE prayers we humbly offer at the throne of heaven, for the sake of our risen and glorified

Lord who ever liveth to make intercession for us and
who hath taught us, when we pray, to say

OUR Father . . .

*Then shall follow the seven Lessons, with Easter hymns
or carols between. The Lessons shall be introduced and
ended with the words given below.*

1st Lesson: Hear what St. Paul saith concerning the
Resurrection of the Lord: 1 Cor. xv. 1–8, 12–22.
Christ is risen from the dead! By death He
hath destroyed death, and life hath He given to all
within the grave.

2nd Lesson: Hear from the Gospels the story of the
Resurrection of our Lord: St. Matthew xxviii.
1–8; St. Mark xvi. 1–7; St. Luke xxiv. 1–9.
Christ is risen from the dead! This is the day
which the Lord hath made: we will rejoice and
be glad in it.

3rd Lesson: Hear further the story of the Resurrec-
tion of our Lord: St. Luke xxiv. 10–12; St.
John xx. 1–10.
Christ is risen from the dead! This is the
Lord's doing, and it is marvellous in our eyes.

4th Lesson: Hear further the story of the Resurrection of our Lord: St. John xx. 11–18.
Christ is risen from the dead! The stone which
the builders rejected is become the head of the
corner.

5th Lesson: Hear the record of the appearance of
our Lord on the road to Emmaus: St. Luke xxiv.
13–35.

Christ is risen from the dead! Still doth the risen Master walk beside us in the way: He enters in and is known to us in the breaking of bread.

6th Lesson: Hear further the story of the Resurrection of our Lord: St. John xx. 19–29.

Christ is risen from the dead! Blessed are they that have not seen, and yet have believed.

7th Lesson: The conclusion of the record of the Resurrection of our Lord: St. John xx. 30, 31; St. Matthew xxviii. 16–20; St. Luke xxiv. 49–53.

Christ is risen from the dead! Arise, shine, for thy light is come, and the glory of the Lord is risen upon thee. Christ is risen from the dead! Thanks be to God who giveth us the victory, through our Lord Jesus Christ.

Then shall be sung the Hymn Te Deum Laudamus (H. 718).

Then an address may be given, and the offerings received.

Then shall the Minister say:

Let us pray.

BLESSED be the God and Father of our Lord Jesus Christ, who according to His abundant mercy hath begotten us again unto a lively hope by the resurrection of Jesus Christ from the dead, to an inheritance incorruptible, undefiled, and that fadeth not away; to whom with Thee, O Father, and Thee, O Holy Spirit, one blessed Trinity, be ascribed all honour, might, majesty and dominion, now and for ever. AMEN.

LOOK down, O Lord, from Thy heavenly throne, illuminate the darkness of this night with Thy celestial brightness, and from the sons of light banish the deeds of darkness; through Jesus Christ our Lord. AMEN.

WE will lay us down in peace and take our rest; for it is Thou Lord only that makest us to dwell in safety. AMEN.

Then shall be sung the hymn Our day of praise is done *or the hymn* Abide with me *and the service shall end with the Blessing:*

NOW the God of peace, that brought again from the dead our Lord Jesus, that great shepherd of the sheep, through the blood of the everlasting covenant, make you perfect in every good work to do His will, working in you that which is well-pleasing in His sight: through Jesus Christ, to whom be glory for ever and ever. And the blessing of God Almighty, Father, Son and Holy Spirit, be amongst you and remain with you always. AMEN.

THE ASCENSION OF OUR LORD

LIFT up your heads, O ye gates; and be ye lift up, ye everlasting doors, and the King of Glory shall come in.

Christ is not entered into the holy places made with hands, but into heaven itself, now to appear in the presence of God for us.

Seeing then that we have a great High Priest, that is passed into the heavens, Jesus the Son of God, let us come boldly unto the throne of grace, that we may obtain mercy, and find grace to help in time of need.

I

ALMIGHTY God, who as at this time didst raise to Thy right hand Thy holy Son, Jesus Christ our Saviour, and hast crowned Him with everlasting glory; we worship and adore Thee in the fellowship of Thy redeemed, and ascribe to Thee and unto the Lamb blessing and honour, glory and power, for ever and ever. AMEN.

MOST Holy Lord, our God, who art of purer eyes than to behold iniquity, but dost not despise the sighing of the contrite; we humbly confess to Thee our great unworthiness. Thou knowest how we have sinned, in departing from Thy ways, in misusing Thy gifts, in rejecting Thy counsels and reproofs, and forgetting Thy claims upon our gratitude and service. Lord, have mercy, and forgive us. Cleanse us from all stain.

Grant to us absolution of all our sins, and deliver

us from the bondage and misery of sin and error. Bring every thought and activity into the obedience of Christ, and so assure us of Thy goodwill and favour, that we may love Thee with all our heart, and know Thy peace which passeth all understanding; through Jesus Christ our Lord. AMEN.

O GOD, who hast created us anew in Christ Jesus, and made us heirs of an incorruptible inheritance; we dedicate ourselves anew to Thee, yielding unto Thee our bodies and our spirits which are Thine. Help us to keep our vows, and to serve Thee in all purity of heart and righteousness of life, to the glory of Thy holy name; through the same Jesus Christ our Lord. AMEN.

O GOD, who hast exalted Thy Son Jesus Christ to Thy right hand, and for the suffering of death hast crowned Him with glory and honour, as King of Saints and High Priest over the House of God; let His intercessions so prevail in our behalf that, setting our affections on things above, we may overcome the world with the victory of faith. Wean our desires from the vanities of earth, and give us grace to have our hearts always lifted up to heaven, where our treasure is. And as Thy well-beloved Son from the depth of His humiliation did pass into the heavens, enable us so to follow Him, with courage and patient endurance, through the sorrows and pains of this mortal life, that, having shared His sufferings here, we may be partakers also of His joy and triumph hereafter; through the same Jesus Christ our Lord, to whom, with Thee the Father, and the Holy Ghost, be glory for ever. AMEN.

II

O GOD, our Father in Heaven; we give Thee thanks and praise for Thy goodness to us at all times and in all places, because Thou hast shielded, rescued, helped, and guided us all the days of our life, and in the multitude of Thy mercies hast brought us to this hour. For the truth we have learned, and the good we have been enabled to do, for the blessings of the past and the hopes of the future, for all that inspires us with trust in Thy wisdom and faithfulness, we bless and praise Thy holy name. But chiefly we thank Thee for Thine unspeakable gift in Jesus Christ Thy Son, our Saviour, and for the life made ours in Him; for the sanctifying and comforting influences of Thy Holy Spirit; for Thy Church, with its ministries of truth and consolation; and for the great and blessed hope of everlasting life.

And this day we rejoice in Thee, and celebrate Thy glorious power and majesty, for that when Thy Son Jesus Christ had purged our sins, Thou didst raise Him from the dead, and set Him at Thy right hand in the heavenly places, far above all principality, and power, and might, and dominion, giving Him the name that is above every name, that in the name of Jesus every knee should bow, and every tongue confess that He is Lord, to the glory of Thee, the Father. Wherefore, with the saints on earth and the redeemed above, we worship and adore, saying, Worthy is the Lamb that was slain to receive power, and riches, and wisdom, and strength, and honour, and glory, and blessing, throughout all ages. AMEN.

O GOD, Almighty Redeemer of men, graciously hear us when we pray for the spread of the Gospel, and for the victory of Thy kingdom in this and in all lands. As Thou didst exalt Thy Son to be a Prince and a Saviour, so do Thou speedily fulfil Thy promise, and give unto Him the heathen for His inheritance and the uttermost parts of the earth for His possession.

Sanctify and increase Thy Church throughout the earth. Remove from it all error, weakness, and division. Enrich its graces and multiply its gifts, and, by the preaching of Thy word and the witness of Thy faithful people, bring all men to the knowledge of Thyself, and to the love and following of Thy Son, our Lord.

O Thou, who rulest the nations in righteousness; we humbly beseech Thee for the government and people of this realm. Preserve and bless our Sovereign Lady Queen Elizabeth, Elizabeth the Queen Mother, Philip, Duke of Edinburgh, Charles, Prince of Wales, and all the Royal Family. Prosper the efforts of our legislators and rulers for the health and welfare of the community. Give us fruitful seasons; advance the cause of learning; purify our commerce and industry from all oppression and injustice; and establish a true and righteous fellowship among men.

O God, who hast given us in Thy Son an High Priest touched with the feeling of our infirmities; hear us when in His name we commend unto Thee Thy sorrowing and suffering children, especially those whom we name in our hearts before Thee . . . the poor, the sick, and the sad, the tempted, and the persecuted, the bereaved, and those drawing near to death. Mercifully forbid that any of Thy suffering children should think themselves forgotten of Thee; but grant that the trial of their faith may be found unto praise and honour and glory, at the appearing of Jesus Christ, their merciful Redeemer.

O Ever-living God, who redeemest the souls of Thy servants; we give Thee thanks for all who, by faith in Thy Son, have accomplished their warfare, and are now at rest; especially for our own beloved, who are now at rest with Thee. . . . Grant unto us who still labour and suffer, that by faith and patience we too may attain to that world of glory whither Thy Son, the forerunner, is for us entered, and, with all the faithful, live in Thy love for ever.

And unto Thee, the Father, with the Son and the Holy Spirit, be glory, as it was in the beginning, is now, and ever shall be, world without end. AMEN.

III

GRANT, we beseech Thee, Almighty God, that like as we do believe Thy only-begotten Son our Lord Jesus Christ to have ascended into the heavens; so we may also in heart and mind thither ascend, and with Him continually dwell, who liveth and reigneth with Thee and the Holy Ghost, one God, world without end. AMEN.

IV

O GOD, the King of Glory, who hast exalted Thine only Son Jesus Christ with great triumph unto Thy kingdom in heaven; we beseech Thee, leave us not comfortless; but send to us Thine Holy Ghost to comfort us, and exalt us unto the same place whither our Saviour Christ is gone before, who liveth and reigneth with Thee and the Holy Ghost, one God, world without end. AMEN.

IT shall come to pass, saith the Lord, that I will pour out My Spirit upon all flesh.

The Spirit itself beareth witness with our spirit, that we are the children of God.

Wilt Thou not revive us again, O Lord, that Thy people may rejoice and be glad in Thee?

I

TO Thee, O God the Father, and to Thee, O Christ, O King exalted, we offer up our due praise and unfeigned thanks, for that Thou hast sent down and dispersed abroad Thy Holy Spirit to restore and renew the spirit of men, to be the first dedication of Thy Church on earth and the first publishing of the Gospel to all lands, the Bond of unity and the Giver of life; to whom with Thee, O Father, and Thee, O Lord Jesus Christ, one blessed Trinity, be ascribed all might, majesty, dominion, and praise, now and ever. AMEN.

GOD of all peace and consolation, who didst gloriously fulfil the great promise of the Gospel by sending down the Holy Ghost on the Day of Pentecost, to establish the Church as the house of His continual presence and power among men; mercifully grant unto us, we beseech Thee, that same gift of the Spirit, to renew, illumine, refresh, and sanctify our souls, to be over us and around us like the light and dew of heaven, and to be in us as a well of water springing up into ever-lasting life; through Jesus Christ our Lord. AMEN.

ALMIGHTY God, all-seeing and all-holy, whose eyes behold the children of men and discern the thoughts and intents of the heart; we are ashamed to lift our eyes to the majesty of Thy glory. We have sinned against Thee through wilfulness and unbelief. We have not sought light through Thy Spirit of wisdom, but, following the counsel of our own will, have erred from Thy way continually. We have not sought strength through Thy Spirit of power; wherefore the good that we would, we have been unable to do, and the evil that we would not, we have done. We have grieved Thy Holy Spirit, and are no more worthy to be called Thy children.

O holy Father, who didst send Thy Spirit to convince of sin and lead to righteousness; we beseech Thee to bring us to repentance, who confess our faults before Thee. Absolve us from our sins; restore to us the peace of the forgiven; and vouchsafe to us Thy Holy Spirit, that we may learn and do Thy perfect will; through Jesus Christ our Lord. AMEN.

ALMIGHTY God, who dost cleanse and sanctify Thy children; hear us as, with lowly hearts, we pray Thee to take possession of the souls Thou hast redeemed, and to perfect Thy work in us. Let Thy Spirit of truth illumine our darkness, that we may understand the deep things of Thy word. Let Thy Spirit of wisdom save us from all false choices, that in Thy light we may see light, and in Thy straight path may not stumble. Let Thy Spirit of purity cleanse us from all stain of evil.

Let Thy Spirit of peace enable us to walk humbly with Thee, and lovingly with each other. Let Thy Spirit of power and love make us strong against temptation, that the fruits of righteousness may abound in our lives. Turn our hearts from the love of the world to the love of Thy will, that we may walk in the way of Thy precepts unto the end; through Jesus Christ our Lord. AMEN.

GOD, who as at this time didst teach the hearts of Thy faithful people, by the sending to them the light of Thy Holy Spirit; grant us by the same Spirit to have a right judgement in all things, and evermore to rejoice in His holy comfort; through the merits of Christ Jesus our Saviour, who liveth and reigneth with Thee, in the unity of the same Spirit, one God, world without end. AMEN.

II

WE praise Thee, O God; we give thanks unto Thee; we adore Thee, the Giver of all good. We bless Thee for the manifold gifts of Thy love, and for the goodness and mercy that have followed us all our days. We praise Thee for the unspeakable gift of Jesus Christ Thy Son, our Saviour. Especially this day we magnify Thy name for the coming of the Holy Spirit, to take of the things of Christ and show them unto His people, and to fulfil in them His work of grace. We bless Thee for the gifts Thou bestowest through Thy Spirit, whereby Thou enablest us to will and to do of Thy good pleasure. With thankful hearts give us obedient wills, and enable us to serve Thee faithfully all the days of our life; through Jesus Christ our Lord, to whom with Thee and the Holy Spirit, be all praise and glory for ever. AMEN.

ALMIGHTY God, who didst send Thy Holy Spirit to abide with Thy Church, to enlighten, comfort, and guide; bestow the same gift unto us, we beseech Thee, to help our infirmities and teach us how to pray.

Regard, we pray Thee, the need of Thy Church, and endue Thy people with power from on high. Enable us so to bear witness to the truth of Thy Gospel, that they who serve Thee may be strengthened, and they who serve Thee not may be convinced of sin, and turn to Thee.

Bestow Thy quickening grace upon Thy Church in this land, that men may know that Thou art in the midst of us, who are called by Thy name. Help us to spread abroad the good news of salvation till all peoples hear it in their own tongue, and incline in their hearts to receive that kingdom which is righteousness, peace, and joy in the Holy Ghost.

God of our fathers, we pray Thee to remember for good the land we love. Strengthen and save the Queen and all her house, and so guide by Thy counsel all in authority under her, that this country may be wisely governed and delivered from affliction, peril, and need. Grant prosperity to our industry and commerce, that peace and well-being may abound throughout the land.

O God, who art love, and whose will for men is peace; quench by the might of Thy Spirit the pride, anger, and greed, which cause man to strive against man, and people against people; prosper those who take counsel together that justice, mercy, and peace may prevail; lead all nations in the ways of good will and common service, and bind the whole human family in one brotherhood, in the kingdom of Thy Son.

Father of mercy, Who knowest the needs of Thy children; we beseech Thee to send the Comforter to all who are in affliction. Strengthen the weak, uphold the sick, refresh the weary, cheer the downcast, and give strong consolation to the sorrowful and the desolate; through Jesus Christ our Lord. AMEN.

WE praise Thee for the whole company of Thy people who, having served Thee and their generation, have fallen asleep in Jesus; especially those dear to us. Give us grace to follow them in faith and patience, so that when this mortal life is ended, we, with them, may see Thy face in Thy heavenly kingdom; through Jesus Christ, our only Saviour, who liveth and reigneth with Thee and the Holy Spirit, one God, blessed for evermore. AMEN.

III

O GOD, who alone art light; send forth now, we beseech Thee, the Spirit of light and understanding in the knowledge of Thy truth, that we may receive into our minds those blessed things which Thou hast made known to us by Jesus Christ our Lord; that we, hearing Thy word with reverence and obedience, may bring forth to Thy praise the fruits of a holy, godly, and loving life; through Jesus Christ our Lord. AMEN.

IV

O LORD Jesus Christ, who didst send from the
Father the Comforter, even the Spirit of
truth; grant that He may enlighten our minds with
the teaching of Thy truth, and sanctify our hearts
with the power of Thy grace, so that, evermore
abiding in Thee, we may be found steadfast in faith
and holy in life, being conformed unto Thine
image; who art with the Father and the Holy
Ghost ever one God, world without end. AMEN.

TRINITY SUNDAY

GOD is love; and he that dwelleth in love, dwelleth in God, and God in him.

Through Christ we have access by one Spirit unto the Father.

Holy, holy, holy, is the Lord God Almighty, which was, and is, and is to come.

I

ETERNAL God, most blessed and most holy, before whom angels veil their faces; with lowly reverence and adoring love we acknowledge the glory of the eternal Trinity, and worship Thee, Father, Son, and Holy Spirit, one God, world without end. Father in heaven, from whom cometh down every good and perfect gift; grant us Thy blessing, and incline Thine ear unto our prayer. Merciful Saviour, who sittest at the right hand of the Father, fulfil Thine own promise, and be present with us who are gathered in Thy name. Holy and life-giving Spirit, help our infirmities, and enable us to worship in the beauty of holiness; and unto Thee, most holy and blessed Trinity, be glory and honour for ever. AMEN.

O LORD our God, we remember our sins before Thee; we cast ourselves upon Thy compassion; we cry unto Thee, Be merciful to us sinners. We have not loved Thee, our Father, with all our heart; we have been unfaithful to our Lord Jesus Christ, our Shepherd and Head; we have grieved the Holy Spirit, the earnest of our inheritance. We have not been pure and holy; we have not been faithful and true; we have been entangled in the world, and overcome of evil.

Father of mercies, forsake not the work of Thine own hands. Be gracious unto us, whom Thou hast redeemed by the precious blood of Christ; take not Thy Holy Spirit from us, who put our whole trust in Thee. Hear us for the sake of Jesus Christ Thy Son, who died for our sins and rose again for our justification, and grant that, obtaining of Thee forgiveness of our sins, and being filled with Thy Holy Spirit, we may hereafter glorify Thee in our body and our Spirit, which are Thine; through the same Jesus Christ our Lord. AMEN.

O GOD, who hast taught us in everything, by prayer and supplication, with thanksgiving, to make our requests known unto Thee; give ear, we beseech Thee, to our prayer, and hearken to the voice of our supplication.

Enable us to love and trust Thee as our heavenly Father; to walk in love, as Thy children; and in all things to honour Thy name and keep Thy commandments.

Make us perfect in Christ Jesus; grant us all to receive of His fullness, and to rest in Him for evermore.

Let the Holy Spirit dwell in us, sanctifying us in spirit and soul and body, and uniting us with all saints in perfect love and eternal joy.

O God, who in the work of man's redemption hast made Thyself known as Father, Son, and Holy Spirit; we beseech Thee to keep us in the faith into which we were baptized; reveal to us the power and riches of Thy grace; and enable us so to glorify Thee in this life, that we may enjoy Thy blessed presence in the world to come, and join with angels and archangels in praising Thee, Father, Son, and Holy Ghost, ever one God, world without end. AMEN.

II

O GIVE thanks unto the Lord, for He is good; for His mercy endureth for ever.

Glory, thanks, and praise be to the Father, holy and eternal, the Father of our Lord Jesus Christ.

Glory, thanks, and praise be to the holy and eternal Son, the Saviour and Redeemer of the world.

Glory, thanks, and praise be to the holy and eternal Spirit, the Renewer, Sanctifier, and Comforter of our souls.

Glory, thanks, and praise be to the blessed and undivided Trinity, one God for evermore.

All Thy works praise Thee, O God; and Thy saints shall bless Thee. Glory and majesty, thanksgiving and praise, be unto Thee, Father, Son, and Holy Spirit, world without end. AMEN.

A LMIGHTY God, who hast made of one blood all nations of men; hear us as we intercede for all mankind.

We pray for Thy holy Church throughout the world, that it may preserve pure and undefiled the faith once delivered to the saints, that one age may praise Thy works to another, and that generations yet unborn may bless Thy holy Name.

We pray for all who minister in holy things, and for those who bear the vessels of the sanctuary, that their hands may be clean and their hearts pure.

We pray for all missionaries, that they may have grace faithfully to declare Thy truth, and turn the heathen from darkness unto light, and from evil unto Thee, the living God.

We pray for Thy people everywhere, that they may stand fast in the faith and walk worthy of their Lord. Grant that, bearing one another's burdens, and esteeming it more blessed to give than to receive, they may live as children of Thee, our Father, obeying the precept of Thy Son our Lord, and keeping the unity of the Spirit in the bond of peace, to the glory of Thy holy Name.

O God, who in time past hast bestowed many and great blessings upon this nation and empire; continue, we beseech Thee, to bless our beloved country, with all its dominions and dependencies. Give abundant grace unto our Sovereign Lady the Queen, that she may reign in righteousness, defend the faith, and seek the advancement of Thy kingdom. Bless all the Royal Family. Endue all in authority throughout the realm with the Spirit of wisdom and understanding, that their endeavours may be directed to the peace and welfare of mankind. And grant that the people of this land, being established in Thy faith and fear, may become a blessing to all nations.

God of all comfort and infinite compassion, who canst turn sorrow into joy; look mercifully upon all who are in trouble, whether of mind, body, or estate; sustain and heal the sick; support and sanctify the dying; visit with Thy mercy those who mourn. Pour Thy divine peace into every wounded spirit; and give to each desolate soul the assurance of Thy love.

O Lord our God, who art the light of the faithful, the strength of them that labour, and the repose of the blessed dead; we thank Thee for all who have faithfully served Thee in their day and generation, into the fruit of whose labours we are entered: we thank Thee for all who rest in Thee, and for all Thy saints upon the earth. And we beseech Thee, grant unto us here present, that we may imitate their good example, faithfully serving Thee in our lives, and being ready at all times to bear witness for Thee, even unto death; through Jesus Christ our Lord, who liveth and reigneth with Thee the Father, and the Holy Ghost, one God, world without end. AMEN.

III

O MERCIFUL God, who hast given us Thy holy word for our learning; grant us ardently to desire, prudently to study, rightly to understand, and perfectly to fulfil the instruction of Thy truth, to the praise of Thy name; through Jesus Christ our Lord. AMEN.

ALMIGHTY and everlasting God, who hast given unto us Thy servants grace by the confession of a true faith to acknowledge the glory of the eternal Trinity, and in the power of the Divine Majesty to worship the Unity; we beseech Thee, that Thou wouldest keep us steadfast in this faith, and evermore defend us from all adversities, who liveth and reignest, one God, world without end. AMEN.

THE COMMEMORATION OF THE FAITHFUL DEPARTED

THE FIRST SUNDAY IN NOVEMBER

THE souls of the righteous are in the hand of God, and there shall no evil touch them. They are in peace.

The righteous shall be had in everlasting remembrance.

Blessed are the pure in heart, for they shall see God. Blessed are the peacemakers, for they shall be called the children of God. Blessed are they that are persecuted for righteousness sake, for theirs is the kingdom of heaven.

I

ALMIGHTY and everlasting God, who hast been in all ages the refuge and strength of Thy people; one generation shall praise Thy works to another, and shall declare Thy mighty acts. We have heard with our ears, O God, our fathers have declared unto us, what work Thou didst in their days, in the times of old. We, their children, now worship and adore Thee, declaring Thy faithfulness and showing forth Thy praise; through Jesus Christ our Lord, to whom with Thee, and the Holy Spirit, one God, be glory and honour, now and ever. AMEN.

O LORD our God, whose compassions fail not; we acknowledge and confess in Thy presence our unworthiness of Thy mercies, and our manifold sins against Thee. We have broken the covenant

Thou madest with our fathers, and didst renew
with us, their children. We have not always walked
by faith in Thy Son our Saviour, or followed
steadfastly in the steps of those who followed Him.
We have been unmindful of their example; we have
been unfaithful to the trust they handed on to us.

Forgive us, we entreat Thee; and by Thy grace
make us worthier of them, and of the inheritance
received from them. Grant that the good we have
seen and felt in them may ever inspire and guide us.
And, seeing we are compassed about with so great
a cloud of witnesses, enable us to lay aside every
weight, and the sin that doth so easily beset us, and
to run with patience the race that is set before us,
looking unto Jesus, the Author and Perfecter of
our faith, that in this present world we may ever be
found faithful, and in the world to come receive the
crown of glory that fadeth not away; through the
same Jesus Christ our Lord. AMEN.

O ALMIGHTY God, who hast knit together
Thine elect in one communion and fellowship,
in the mystical body of Thy Son Jesus Christ our
Lord; grant us grace so to follow Thy blessed saints
in all virtuous and godly living, that we may come to
those unspeakable joys which Thou hast prepared
for them that unfeignedly love Thee; through the
same Jesus Christ our Lord, who liveth and reigneth
with Thee and the Holy Spirit, one God, world
without end. AMEN.

II

O GOD, who hast founded Thy Church upon
earth, and hast revealed Thy loving-kindness
and truth from age to age; we pray Thee to enrich
Thy people everywhere with Thy heavenly grace.

Keep them true to the heritage of faith received from those who have gone before; enable them to serve Thee in righteousness and godly fear; bring them into one brotherhood of faith and love, and keep them in communion with all Thy saints in heaven.

We beseech Thee to bless Thy Church in our native land. Pour out Thy Spirit upon all its members, that, cherishing the traditions received from their fathers, they may yet be ready to follow the light which Thou shalt give, and to make new ventures of faith as Thou shalt call.

Crown with Thy blessing our Sovereign Lady the Queen, and all the Royal House. Guide with Thy wisdom the Queen's ministers and counsellors, that under their rule and guidance Thy people may lead just and peaceable lives in all godliness and honesty.

Father of all, whose mercies are infinite; we beseech Thee to bring back to Thy fold those who are wandering from Thee, and to shed Thy light on all who are in darkness. Look in Thy tender pity on the sick and the suffering, the aged and the weary, all who are in sorrow or distress; and especially on those whom we name in our hearts before Thee, beseeching Thee to pour into every wounded heart the comfort of Thy love; through Jesus Christ our Lord. AMEN.

ETERNAL Father, who art the God not of the dead but of the living; we give Thee thanks and praise for all the generations of the faithful, who, having served Thee here in godliness and love, are now with Thee in glory.

We thank Thee for those who have enriched the world with truth and beauty; for the wise and good of every land and age, who by teaching and life have given light to their fellow men. We bless Thee for those who have laboured and made sacrifice for freedom, good government, and equal laws; for those who won the liberty of faith and worship in which we live; and for those who have brought blessing to others by Their charity and good works. We thank Thee for the apostles and martyrs of our holy faith; and for those who suffered for the sake of Christ. And for the splendour of all heroic deeds and the grace of all holy lives, we praise and bless Thy name.

With gratitude we call to remembrance those whom we have known and honoured; those who taught us by word and guided us by example, and, most of all, those who loved us, and shielded and helped us; fathers and mothers, and all the dear kindred of our homes, whose faces we see no more, but who are precious to us for ever. . . .

Grant us firmly to believe and assuredly to know that we are still one with them in holy fellowship; and enable us so to follow them in all godly living and faithful service, that hereafter we may with them behold Thy face in glory, and in the heavenly places be one with them for ever; through Jesus Christ our Lord, who liveth and reigneth, and is worshipped and glorified, with Thee, O Father, and the Holy Spirit, world without end. AMEN.

III

O LORD our God, who hast given Thy word to teach us truth and build us up in righteousness; open our hearts to Thy wisdom and love, subdue all discord within us, and let Thy holy

Spirit so guide us that in Thy light we may see light, and have grace to follow whithersoever it may lead; through Jesus Christ our Lord. AMEN.

IV

ALMIGHTY God, who hast manifested Thy love and power in the life and death of Thy redeemed and holy ones of old; grant that, like them, we may have grace to glorify Thee, loving Thee whom they have loved, and finding Thee whom they have found, and may come at the last to dwell with them and with Thee, for ever, in the joy of Thy glorious presence; through Jesus Christ our Lord. AMEN.

ST. ANDREW'S DAY

30TH NOVEMBER

If St. Andrew's Day is observed on the first Sunday in Advent, use should also be made of the service for that day.

IF I forget thee, O Jerusalem, let my right hand forget her cunning.

Seek the Lord God of your fathers, and do His commandments.

The righteous shall be had in everlasting remembrance. The memory of the just is blessed.

I

ALMIGHTY God, who hast made known Thy mercies to our fathers in every age, and hast continued them to us their children; vouchsafe Thy presence, we beseech Thee, unto us, and to our kindred beyond the seas who are this day near to us in spirit; help us all to wait upon Thee in humble faith and adoration, and grant that our prayers and theirs may find acceptance with Thee; through Jesus Christ our Lord. AMEN.

ALMIGHTY and most merciful Father, we humbly confess our manifold sins and shortcomings. We acknowledge our transgressions as a nation and people: our pride and vainglory, our self-sufficiency and forgetfulness of Thee. We have been unthankful for Thy great goodness to us. We have been slow to obey Thy command to make disciples of all nations. We have broken the unity of Thy Church, and by our divisions have weakened Thy cause and hindered the Gospel of Christ.

Blot out our transgressions, O Lord, we beseech Thee. Revive Thy work in the midst of the years, and cause Thy power and glory to be seen in the sanctuary, as in the days of old; through Jesus Christ our Lord. AMEN.

O LORD God, who hast given us a noble inheritance in the Scottish name; enable us to hold fast the faith which Thou gavest unto our fathers, and hast preserved through centuries of suffering and trial. Keep us true to the vision of life Thou hast revealed in Thy dear Son; lead us in the paths of uprightness and truth; and grant that, guided always by Thy Spirit, and trusting in Thy love, we may abide in fellowship one with another, and all in fellowship with Thee; through Jesus Christ our Lord. AMEN.

A LMIGHTY God, who didst give such grace to Thy Apostle Saint Andrew, that he counted the sharp and painful death of the Cross to be an high honour, and a great glory; grant us to take and esteem all troubles and adversities which shall come unto us for Thy sake, as things profitable for us toward the obtaining of everlasting life; through Jesus Christ our Lord. AMEN.

If in Advent, the following may be added:

A LMIGHTY God, give us grace that we may cast away the works of darkness, and put upon us the armour of light, now in the time of this mortal life, in which Thy Son Jesus Christ came to visit us in great humility; that in the last day, when He shall come again in His glorious majesty to judge both the quick and the dead, we may rise to the life immortal; through Him who liveth and reigneth with Thee, and the Holy Ghost, now and ever. AMEN.

II

GREAT and marvellous are Thy works, Lord God Almighty; just and true are Thy ways, Thou King of saints.

We have heard with our ears, our fathers have declared unto us, what work Thou didst in their days, in the times of old.

We bless Thee for the land Thou gavest unto our fathers, for the mountains and rivers they loved and named, and for the patience and hope with which they laboured to make the land yield her increase. We thank Thee that we inherit cities we have not builded, and fields and forests we have not planted, through Thy blessing on their toil.

We thank Thee for all who throughout the generations have suffered, toiled, and died for our beloved land. We praise Thee for the faith of the apostle, the constancy of the martyr, the zeal of the reformer, the courage of the warrior, and for the heritage they have left us. Most of all for Thine unspeakable gift, Jesus Christ Thy Son, with whom Thou dost freely give us all things, we praise and adore Thee, through Him, our Lord and Saviour, who, with Thee and the Holy Spirit, is worshipped and glorified, one God, world without end. AMEN.

O ALMIGHTY God, look mercifully upon the whole world, redeemed by the blood of Thy dear Son. Send forth Thy light and truth, that souls who know Thee not may turn to Thee, and Thy glorious triumph be hastened by the perfecting of Thy people.

Bless Thy Church, Catholic and Apostolic. Let peace be within her walls. Cast out all that offends, and kindle Thy love and power in the hearts of all Thy people.

We beseech Thee to bless every endeavour to fulfil the charge committed to Thy Church, to be Thy witness in this and other lands. Grant that as Saint Andrew brought his brother to Jesus, so we, like him, may be ever diligent in Thy service, striving to lead our brethren unto Thee, and to bring wanderers to Thy fold.

Let Thy grace rest upon those who labour in Thy cause in distant lands. Protect them in danger; endue them with zeal and love, that they may turn many to righteousness. Hasten the time when the fullness of the Gentiles shall be gathered in, and all Israel be saved.

We pray for the British Commonwealth of Nations. Bless Thy servant Queen Elizabeth, her Royal House, and all in authority under her. Defend the Navy, Army, and Air Force in all times of danger. Bless those who till the fields, those engaged in trade and commerce, and all who go down to the sea in ships. Make the Empire strong and great in righteousness and in the fear of Thy holy name.

O God, who hast sent our people to sow beside all waters, and to multiply sure dwellings on the earth, hear our prayers for our friends and kindred who are far away, and for all whom we this day remember before Thee in the silence of our hearts. . . . Grant that none of us may add to the burdens of those who love us by forgetfulness, silence, or delay; and give us all to know that the eternal God is our refuge, and underneath are the everlasting arms.

O Lord of light and peace, grant courage and patience to those who are troubled in mind or body. Relieve their sufferings, surround them with loving care, and suffer no one to add to their grief.

We pray for the young, and for those who teach them. Grant, O God, that they may be led by precept and example in the old paths, where is the good way, and be taught that fear of Thee which is the beginning of wisdom; and may no failure of ours obscure for them the vision of Thy will.

O Lord Most High, we bless and praise Thy holy name for all who have served Thee faithfully in this life, and are now at rest. In especial we thank Thee for those dear to us, who have loved and shielded and guided us in days gone by, and whom we hold in loving memory before Thee. Keep us united with them in the communion of Thy saints; enable us to follow them in faithfulness and love; and bring us at the last with them to the joy and glory of Thy heavenly kingdom.

Glory be to the Father, and to the Son, and to the Holy Ghost; as it was in the beginning, is now, and ever shall be, world without end. AMEN.

III

O GOD, who by the preaching of the Apostles didst cause the light of Thy Gospel to shine upon the nations; grant, we beseech Thee, that we, having their life and labour in remembrance, may show forth our thankfulness to Thee for so great a gift, by following the example of their zeal and service; through Jesus Christ our Lord. AMEN.

IV

ALMIGHTY God, who didst give such grace unto Thy holy Apostle Saint Andrew, that he readily obeyed the calling of Thy Son Jesus Christ, and followed Him without delay; grant unto us all, that we, being called by Thy holy word, may forthwith give up ourselves obediently to fulfil Thy holy commandments; through the same Jesus Christ our Lord. AMEN.

THANKSGIVING FOR HARVEST

THE earth is the Lord's, and the fullness thereof; the world and they that dwell therein.

God left not Himself without witness, in that He did good, and gave you rain from heaven and fruitful seasons, filling your hearts with food and gladness.

O bless our God, ye people, and make the voice of His praise to be heard; which holdeth our soul in life, and suffereth not our feet to be moved.

I

ALMIGHTY God, our heavenly Father, the eyes of all wait upon Thee, and Thou givest them their meat in due season. That Thou givest them they gather; Thou openest Thine hand, and they are satisfied with good. We glorify Thee that Thou hast again fulfilled Thy gracious promise, that while the earth remaineth, seed-time and harvest shall not cease. For the seasons of the ever-changing year we thank Thee; for the beauty of earth and sky and sea. For cloud and sunshine, for rain and wind fulfilling Thy word; for flower and fruit and tree, and now for the bounteous harvest, we praise Thee, O God.

And forasmuch as without Thee labour is vain, we thank Thee for Thy blessing upon the skill and diligence of those who ploughed the earth and sowed the seed, and now have reaped the fruit of their toil. Thou hast crowned the year with Thy goodness. O Lord, our Lord, how excellent is Thy name in all the earth.

Fill us with thankfulness for all Thy temporal gifts; and since it is not by bread alone that man doth live, grant us evermore to give thanks to Thee for Him who is the true bread that came down from heaven, even Jesus Christ our Lord. AMEN.

O MERCIFUL Father, the remembrance of Thy goodness humbles us with the consciousness of our unworthiness and sin. We have been disobedient children and unprofitable servants. We have too often received Thy gifts with little gratitude, and used them with little care. Forgetting Thy promises, we have been filled with anxious thought, lest Thy faithfulness should fail or Thy mercies cease.

O God, we beseech Thee, forgive our offences. Grant us assurance of reconciliation, and fill us with joy and peace in believing; through Jesus Christ our Lord. AMEN.

O GOD, who by Thy gracious providence hast made the earth to bring forth her fruits for the use of man, and caused them to be gathered for the comfort of Thy creatures; keep us mindful of our dependence upon Thee, and deepen our trust in Thy fatherly care. Give us grace to use Thy bountiful gifts to Thy glory, to the relief of those who are needy, and to our own good. Grant that, enjoying them in wisdom, temperance, and thankfulness, we may ever be mindful to seek the spiritual food of Thy word, wherewith our souls are nourished unto life everlasting. And grant that we, abiding in Christ as branches of the true Vine, may daily bring forth the fruits of the Spirit, to the honour of Thy holy name.

And to Thee, O Father, with the Son and the Holy Spirit, be honour and glory for ever and ever. AMEN.

II

O LORD our God, Creator of all men, who makest Thy sun to rise on the evil and the good, and sendest rain on the just and the unjust; we beseech Thee to visit the whole earth with righteousness, and Thy people with salvation, and to turn the disobedient to the wisdom of the just.

Let Thy Spirit be outpoured upon Thy Church in every land, and especially in this land of our birth and love. Bless the words and works of Thy servants who have gone forth into the field of the world, bearing the precious seed of Thy kingdom. Help them to sow in faith, nothing doubting, that they may reap in joy; and if at times they sow in tears, be pleased in due season to bring them again with rejoicing, bearing their sheaves with them.

Send forth more labourers into Thy harvest, and hasten the time when the fullness of the Gentiles shall be gathered in, and all Israel be saved.

Almighty God, by whom kings reign and princes decree justice, and from whom alone come wisdom and understanding; guide always and bless our Sovereign Lady the Queen, and grant Thy heavenly counsel to her ministers of state, and to all who give themselves to the public service. Bless our land with honourable industry, pure manners, and true religion. In time of prosperity fill all hearts with thankfulness, and if trouble come, suffer not our trust in Thee to fail. Continue Thy favour towards us, that the earth may yield its increase, and that we may be a people fearing Thee and doing righteousness.

Hear us as we pray for all who labour in the service of their fellows, and especially those who gather, in their seasons, the kindly fruits of the earth and the harvest of the seas; that they may remember Thee, from whom every good gift cometh, and worship, and give Thee thanks.

O God, whose blessed Son healed all manner of sickness and disease among the people; continue His gracious work in the homes and hospitals of our land. Grant that all physicians, surgeons, and nurses may have the mind that was in Christ Jesus, and receive Thy heavenly aid in their ministrations.

Comfort and sustain those who are in trouble, whether of body, mind, or estate. Defend the weak, the needy, the afflicted, the widowed, and the fatherless.

We pray for all whom we love, that they and we may be joined in bonds which shall not be broken, in Jesus Christ our Lord. AMEN.

ETERNAL God, the Father of our Lord Jesus Christ, we praise Thee that Thou didst raise Him from the dead, the first-fruits of them that slept. We thank Thee for all, especially those dear to our own hearts, who, having fallen asleep in Him, are now alive for evermore. Raise us, through faith in Him, from the death of sin unto the life of righteousness, that when we depart this life, this corruptible may put on incorruption, and this mortal put on immortality, and death be swallowed up in victory; through Jesus Christ our Lord, who liveth and reigneth with Thee and the Holy Spirit, world without end. AMEN.

III

ALMIGHTY God, who hast given us the fruits of the earth in their season; keep us ever mindful that Thou hast given us also the spiritual food of Thy word. Grant us now and always to receive it in humble faith, that our souls may be nourished unto life eternal; through Jesus Christ our Lord. AMEN.

IV

O LORD of the harvest and Giver of our daily bread, we rejoice in all Thy fatherly goodness; and pray that Thy loving-kindness may so prevail in the hearts of Thy children everywhere, that the earth may be filled with gladness and peace; through Jesus Christ our Lord. AMEN.

LECTIONARY

	Old Testament	Epistle	Gospel
1st Sunday in Advent	2 Sam. **7**. 4–16	Rom. **13**. 8–14	{ Mark **13**. 1–13 or Luke **21**. 26–33
	or Isa. **1**. 10–18	Rom. **13**. 8–14	Matt. **21**. 1–9
2nd ,, ,,	Isa. **11**. 1–10	Rom. **15**. 4–13	Mark **13**. 24–37
	or Isa. **5**. 1–7	Rom. **15**. 4–13	Matt. **25**. 1–13
3rd ,, ,,	Micah **5**. 2 and Zech **9**. 9–10	1 Cor. **3**. 16; **4**. 5	Matt. **11**. 2–10
	or Isa. **51**. 1–8	1 Cor. **3**. 16; **4**. 5	Matt. **13**. 14–52
4th ,, ,,	{ Isa. **9**. 2–7 (R.V.) or Isa. **54**. 1–10	Phil. **4**. 4–9	{ John **1**. 19–28 or Matt. **3**. 1–12
	or Isa. **33**. 1–8	Phil. **4**. 4–9	{ Luke **1**. 68–79 Luke **3**. 1–14
Christmas Eve	{ Isa. **9**. 2–7 (R.V.) or Isa. **23**. 5–8	Rom. **1**. 1–6	Matt **1**. 18–23
Christmas Day	Isa. **9**. 2–7 (R.V.)	Titus **2**. 11; **3**. 7	Luke **2**. 1–20
Sunday after Christmas	Isa. **40**. 1–11	Heb. **1**. 1–12	John **1**. 1–18
Last Sunday in the Year or New Year's Eve	Deut. **8**.	2 Pet. **3**. 8–14	Luke **12**. 32–40
New Year's Day or First Sunday in the New Year	Deut. **11**. 1–12	Phil. **3**. 7–15	Matt. **6**. 19–33
Epiphany	{ Isa. **60**. 1–12 or Isa. **61**	Eph. **2**. 11–18	Matt. **2**. 1–12
1st Sunday in Lent	Isa. **58**. 1–8	1 John **2**. 7–17	Matt. **4**. 1–11
	or Isa. **1**. 10–18	2 Tim. **3**. 14; **4**. 8	Luke **4**. 1–13
2nd ,, ,,	{ Isa. **59**. 1–8 or Genesis **8**	1 Thess. **4**. 1–8	{ Matt. **15**. 21–8 or Matt. **17**. 1–9
	or { Isa. **59**. 9–15 or Gen. **40**	Rom. **2**. 1–10	Matt. **16**. 21–8
3rd ,, ,,	{ Jer. **7**. 1–11 or Gen. **11**. 1–9	Acts **12**. 1–11	{ Matt. **21**. 33–46 or Luke **13**. 31–5
	or { Jer. **18**. 1–10 or Gen. **42**. 1–21	Eph. **5**. 1–14	{ Luke **11**. 14–28 or Matt. **20**. 17–28
4th ,, ,,	{ Jer. **26**. 1–16 or Gen. **13**. 1–12	Heb. **12**. 22–9	{ John **6**. 1–14 or Matt. **18**. 15–22
	or { Jer. **31**. 1–9 or Gen. **45**. 1–18	Phil. **3**. 7–15	{ John **8**. 1–11 or John **2**. 3–22

	Old Testament	Epistle	Gospel
5th Sunday in Lent —Passion Sunday	Isa. **63.** 1–9	Heb. **9.** 11–22	John **6.** 27–35 or John **10.** 7–18
	or Isa. **59.** 16–21	Heb. **9.** 11–22	John **8.** 46–59 or Matt. **12.** 14–21
6th Sunday in Lent —Palm Sunday	Zech. **9.** 9–14	Phil. **2.** 5–11	John **12.** 1–16 or Matt. **21.** 1–11 and/or Matt. **27.** 1–54
Monday before Easter	Isa. **42.** 1–12	1 Cor. **1.** 18–25	Matt. **21.** 12–17 or John **12.** 1–9 or Mark **14.** 1–72
Tuesday ,, ,,	Zech. **13**	Eph. **2.** 12–22	Matt. **21.** 23–32 or Mark **12.** 1–12 or Mark **15.** 1–39
Wednesday ,, ,,	Isa. **63.** 7–19	1 John **4.** 7–11	Mark **14.** 1–11 or Luke **22.** 1–71
Thursday ,, ,,	Isa. **50.** 4–11	1 Cor. **11.** 17–34	John **13.** 1–17 or Matt. **26.** 17–30 or Luke **23.** 1–49
Good Friday	Isa. **52.** 13; **53.** 5	Heb. **10.** 1–25	Matt. **27.** 33–50 or John **19.** 1–37
Holy Saturday	Hos. **6.** 1–6	1 Pet. **3.** 17–22	John **19.** 38–42 or Matt. **27.** 57–66
Easter Day	Exod. **12.** 1–14	Col. **3.** 1–11	St. Mark **16.** 1–15 or John **20.** 1–18
	or Isa. **25.** 1–9	Rev. **1.** 10–18	Luke **24.** 1–12
Ascensiontide	2 Kings **2.** 1–15	Acts **1.** 1–11	Luke **24.** 44–53
	or Dan **7.** 9–14	Heb. **4.** 9–16	Matt. **28.** 16–20
Whitsunday	Isa. **11.** 1–10	Acts **2.** 1–11	John **3.** 16–21
	or Isa. **61.** 1–3	Acts **10.** 34–48a	John **14.** 15–31
Trinity Sunday	Isa. **6.** 1–8	Rev. **4.** 1–11	John **3.** 1–15
	or Dan. **8.** 9–14	Rev. **4.** 1–11	John **4.** 1–26
All Saints' Day	Isa. **51.** 1–11	Rev. **7.** 9–17 or Heb. **11.** 32; **12.** 2	Matt. **5.** 1–12
St. Andrew's Day	Isa. **49.** 1–12	Rom. **10.** 4–17	John **1.** 35–42a
Harvest Thanksgiving	Deut. **26.** 1–11 or Isa. **55.** 9–13	Gal. **6.** 6–10	Luke **12.** 13–34

PRINTED IN GREAT BRITAIN
AT THE UNIVERSITY PRESS, OXFORD
BY VIVIAN RIDLER
PRINTER TO THE UNIVERSITY

THE APOSTLES' CREED

I BELIEVE in God the Father Almighty, Maker of heaven and earth:

And in Jesus Christ His only Son our Lord, Who was conceived by the Holy Ghost, Born of the Virgin Mary, Suffered under Pontius Pilate, Was crucified, dead, and buried, He descended into hell; The third day He rose again from the dead, He ascended into heaven, And sitteth on the right hand of God the Father Almighty; From thence He shall come to judge the quick and the dead.

I believe in the Holy Ghost; The holy Catholic Church; The Communion of Saints; The Forgiveness of sins; The Resurrection of the body; And the Life everlasting. AMEN.